中国年度
酒单大奖

中国葡萄酒餐厅指南

— 2014 —

中国年度酒单大奖评委会　撰

北京出版集团公司
北京美术摄影出版社

序

Peter Forrestal
评审团和最高评审委员会联合主席
Co-Chairman of Judges & the Supreme Panel

"第二届中国年度酒单大奖"如约而至，我们欣喜地看到进步无处不在。报名餐厅的成倍增加更是让我们切实地感受到第一届大奖带来的影响力。大奖评委和授予优秀酒单杯数的最高评委会肯定了参与酒单所取得的进步。越来越多的侍酒师认识到年份很关键，而优秀的侍酒师开始关注每款酒的质量以保持酒单的平衡。评委亦强调了从酒单中剔除劣质酒款的重要性，而有些参选餐厅还没有意识到这与选择最好的酒款是同样重要的。

最佳美食和美酒搭配葡萄酒酒单不断创新，今年有三家候选餐厅获得进一步向大众展示其水平的机会。由专业评委到餐厅试吃，品尝主厨拿手菜与美酒的搭配。而大众则通过在线观看试吃纪录片，投票选出他们的心中最爱。

我们非常高兴看到更多的中国葡萄酒出现在酒单上，并期望这个趋势能愈发明显。随着本土企业的发展，中国侍酒师应该摒弃成见，骄傲地向来自四面八方的消费者展示产自中国的葡萄酒。

中国最佳酒单足以与世界最佳相提并论。我们欣慰地见到27家获得特别奖项的酒单优势明显且风格不一。这使得评选特别奖项的难度越来越大。这样的进步将会让中国最佳餐厅、酒吧和会所的消费者都受益匪浅。

As we have moved into the second year of China's Wine List of the Year Awards, we have been heartened by the progress that has been made. The number of entries has doubled and so the impact of the first year's work has spread.

The judges and the members of the Supreme Panel, who rank the finalists, have commented on the significant improvement in the standard of entries. Increasingly, sommeliers are realizing the importance of identifying the vintage of all wines on their list and the best are being even more careful about the quality of wines they feature. The judges did sound a word of warning about the importance of pruning poor quality wines from lists. Some overlook that this needs to be as thoroughly done as selecting the best available wines.

The Food and Wine Matching Award has taken a step forward this year with the three finalists given the opportunity to demonstrate their talents. Expert judges took part in the trials and enjoyed the matching of wines to some of the chef's finest dishes. Members of the public were able to view film of the trial on line and vote for their favourite.

We were particularly happy to see more Chinese wines on the best lists — and look forward to seeing this trend becoming even more noticeable. As the local industry develops, Chinese sommeliers need to show their pride by sharing these wines with locals and international visitors.

The best lists in China rank with the finest in the world. We are delighted to see greater strength, more diversity and depth, in the top 27 lists which were entered for the Awards. Selecting the top half dozen as finalists was a demanding task. The customers in China's finest restaurants, wine bars and clubs will all benefit from this improvement.

Rob Hirst
国际酒单大奖创办人
中国年度酒单大奖创办人
Founder of Wine list of the Year Awards
Founder of China's Wine list of the Year Awards

欢迎阅读《中国葡萄酒餐厅指南 2014》，这本指南罗列了在中国所有获得"2014 中国年度酒单大奖"的优秀餐厅、酒店、俱乐部和酒吧。

这是中国第一个专业的酒单大奖，所有的奖项均由三组 30 多位评审依顺序层层筛选、评论而评选出来。30 多位评审囊括了中国及国际上知名的侍酒师大师、葡萄酒大师及葡萄酒界权威人士；通过与中国侍酒师协会的紧密合作，大奖已成功举办两届，认可并表彰了中国优秀的侍酒师们；并宣告世界，中国优秀的酒单已达到了世界级水准。

中国年度酒单大奖是对中国最佳葡萄酒酒单的认可和奖励，它不仅认可、表彰那些倾注了心血与精力制作酒单的侍酒师们，也是对投资这本酒单的餐饮机构的认可与鼓励。

再次恭贺所有获奖者们！

Welcome to China's Wine Restaurant Guide for 2014 which recognises the outstanding Restaurants, Hotels, Clubs and Wine Bars across China who have been successful in the 2014 China's Wine List of the Year Awards.

These Awards, China's first such Awards, are judged by three independent panels of over 30 judges from across China and the World including Master Sommeliers and Masters of Wine, and were established - with China's National Sommelier Competition - to find and celebrate China's best sommelier's and the product of their endeavours - their great wine lists.

China's Wine List of the Year Awards are designed to ensure the most outstanding wine and beverage lists across China - big and small - are given due recognition and reward for the great skill and experience of their Sommeliers plus the dedicated investment of resources by the Restaurants, International Hotels, Wine Bars, and Clubs that produce them — congratulations to all Glass and Award winners!

Tommy Lam
亚洲葡萄酒学会总裁
中国侍酒师大赛创办人

随着第二届的评选开始，我们欣慰地看到报名餐厅的进步。大多数的酒单都展现出侍酒师的学识以及参与评选的自信。整个酒单的档次不断提高，对杯卖酒单部分也愈发重视。与此同时，侍酒师们也开始表现出对国产酒，尤其是优质国产酒的自信，并向消费者们推广。

毫无疑问，中国最佳酒单已然能与世界顶级酒单相提并论。酒单大奖向世界展示着属于它们的光彩。

As we have moved into the second year's judging of China's Wine List of the Year, the progress made has been the source of much delight. With many lists, it is clear that Sommeliers have learnt a great deal and gained confidence from the experience of being involved in the Awards. Standards of presentation have risen, more emphasis is being placed on lists by the glass, and Sommeliers are showing more national pride by celebrating China's own, increasingly impressive wines.

There is no question that the best wine lists of China deserve to be ranked among the world's finest. These Awards show them to the world in all their splendour.

梅宁博
酒斛网主编

作为一名葡萄酒媒体人，我经常会被读者朋友问到此类问题："我想请朋友吃饭，哪个餐厅的酒单比较好，酒的价格又实惠？"、"我要到北京出差了，你可以推荐哪些好的餐厅？"、"情人节要到了，我想去一个环境浪漫的餐厅里喝香槟，哪里比较好？"于是，我们在 2013 年产生了"寻找中国最佳餐厅酒单"的想法。而此时，中国侍酒师行业的前辈 Tommy Lam 先生又介绍我们认识了"国际酒单大奖"的创办人 Rob Hirst 先生。来自澳大利亚的 Rob 在当地从事了 20 余年的餐厅酒单评选工作。我们的理念不谋而合，并决定共同举办"中国年度酒单大奖"。一方面，旨在找到国内最好的餐厅酒单，并分享给更多喜爱美食美酒的读者；另一方面，我们也希望通过这样的活动，提升国内餐厅对葡萄酒酒单的重视度。

今年，我们成功举办了"第二届中国年度酒单大奖"。参加评选的餐厅覆盖全国 30 个城市，达到了 286 家之多。最终，"2014 中国年度酒单大奖"花落上海的"Napa Wine Bar & Kitchen"。

我们惊讶于餐厅参加评选的积极态度、餐饮和葡萄酒业内同行的关注及肯定。为了更好地服务读者，我们决定将大奖的评选结果以书籍的形式出版，使之成为一本读者选择餐厅的工具书，做到随手可查、随时预订。于是，《中国葡萄酒餐厅指南 2014》诞生了。

这本书不仅刊登了全国 23 个城市的 138 个获奖餐厅、7 家航空公司的用餐特色和酒单介绍，还有来自酒单大奖国际评委的专业点评。这将最大程度地解决读者朋友们在选择餐厅时无从下手的问题。对于商务人士，我们还专门从各大国际航空公司的头等舱和商务舱之中，评选出最佳的酒单，希望您在旅途中也有美食和美酒的陪伴！

最后，我要衷心感谢所有酒斛网读者长期以来的支持；感谢我们的出版人 Simon Fann 先生，在他的努力下，这本书才得以出版。最后更要感谢中国年度酒单大奖的国际评审团队！我们将继续秉承"为美食和美酒爱好者服务"的理念，为读者朋友们提供更多专业、实用的信息。

由来和主旨

《中国葡萄酒餐厅指南 2014》收录了"2014 中国年度酒单大奖"所有的获奖餐厅、酒店、俱乐部和酒吧。

中国年度酒单大奖由已成功举办 20 届"澳大利亚年度酒单大奖"的国际酒单大奖组织和酒斛网 (www.vinehoo.com) 联合举办,获得了中国侍酒师协会(筹)鼎力支持。

中国年度酒单大奖是对中国侍酒师用精力和心血制作的酒单的认可和奖励,旨在通过对酒单的评级,寻找到最优秀的餐厅、酒吧和俱乐部,为消费者提供通往最佳酒单的"路线地图"。

中国年度酒单大奖主办方——国际酒单大奖组织邀请了国际顶级葡萄酒专家参与"2014 中国年度酒单大奖"的评审工作。评审团由两位联合主席 Tommy LAM(林志帆)先生和现任澳大利亚年度酒单大奖的评委主席 Peter FORRESTAL 先生统筹安排评审工作。由 30 多位专家组成的顶级评审团包括:世界最佳侍酒师兼葡萄酒及侍酒师大师证书拥有者 Gerard BASSET、世界侍酒师工会首席执行官兼侍酒师大师 Brian JULYAN 以及来自美国的世界知名侍酒师大师、作家兼教育家 Evan GOLDSTEIN、葡萄酒大师 Andrew CAILLARD 和葡萄酒大师 Ned GOODWIN。中国地区的评审团包括:上海的齐仲蝉(Chantal CHI)、郝利文(Martin HAO);北京的 Jim BOYCE、陆江(Maxime LU)、Richard XU;香港的 Thomas CHUNG;台湾的 John HUNG;澳门的 David WONG;20 余位专业在职侍酒师。这个全球知名的国际评审团确保了中国年度酒单大奖的权威性,而其评选结果将为那些寻求优秀酒单的消费者提供非常宝贵的指南。

酒单评选步骤及奖项含义

评选步骤:

一

在审查完报名酒单的真实性后,评审团将会评选出优秀的酒单,授予一杯奖、二杯奖或三杯奖的奖项,这些奖项标志着该获奖餐厅酒单已经达到和世界最佳葡萄酒单相当的实力;

二

评委将会为每个酒单提供一份点评,不仅为消费者提供参考,而且为侍酒师们提高酒单质量提供了宝贵的建议;

三

27 个特别奖项亦会从此获奖名单中脱颖而出,分别表彰获得 27 个特别奖项的酒店餐厅、独立餐厅、俱乐部及酒吧。

奖项含义:

被推荐的酒单

优秀的酒单

卓越的酒单

Mr Gian Luca Fusetto

餐厅介绍

8 1/2 Otto e Mezzo BOMBANA 餐厅是米其林三星世界名厨 Umberto Bombana 继香港店取得巨大成功后在中国大陆地区的首个餐厅项目。坐落于上海独特的地标场所洛克外滩源。坐揽浦江两岸的唯芯美景，名厨 Bombana 带领他充满激情的团队为食客们创作最高水平的顶级嘉大利美食。行政主厨 Riccardo La Pema 精选来自世界各地的食材。让客人在美食中感受意大利的美妙风光。意大利总经理兼侍酒师 Gian Luca Fusetto 独家挑选的 500 多个葡萄酒酒品种，为美酒爱好者创造了又一顶级的味蕾盛享。

2014 年度酒单奖项

菜式

价格标示

8 1/2 OTTO E MEZZO BOMBANA SHANGHAI

  最佳单一国家葡萄酒酒单

2014 年度特别奖项

鉴于本书收录来自中国的餐饮机构，币种有以下几种：RMB 人民币 / HKD 港币 / MOP 澳门币 / TWD 新台币

酒单大奖专家评审团之酒单点评：

一切都源于意大利 — 从华丽的装潢到完美的菜单和酒单。意大利经营酒庄。老年份顶级酒款和众多大瓶装都是其特色。尽管其他产区也有所涉猎。意大利酒仍是当之无愧的霸主。

A dazzling showcase of all things Italian – from the sumptuous décor to the superb menu and glittering wine list. There are feature pages for elite Italian producers, with back vintages of top wines plus a selection of magnums. While most countries are represented, the focus is undeniably Italian.

专家酒单点评

意式

人均消费　RMB1000
葡萄酒价格　$ $ $
酒单酒款数　500
杯卖酒款　18
杯卖酒价格　RMB90-450
开 瓶 费　RMB450/ 餐厅购酒可免开瓶费
酒单撰写人　Mr Gian Luca Fusetto
电　话　86 21 60872890
营业时间　18:00 - 23:00
　　　　　11:00 - 15:00（周日早午餐）
地　址　上海市黄浦区圆明园路协进大楼
网　址　www.ottoebombana.com/shanghai

以餐厅实际收取为准

11

为了方便读者出行。酒斛网（www.vinehoo.com）将获奖餐厅信息刊登在网站上。如有需要，请扫描左侧二维码登录网站查阅。

编者话

田燕东

作为一名侍酒师出身的葡萄酒从业人员，我常会被朋友问到"哪家餐厅有好的酒单"、"哪家酒吧有好的杯卖葡萄酒"等问题。我开始思索，中国城市如此之多，餐厅又多如牛毛，如何将所有优秀葡萄酒餐厅的信息进行整合，并以一本指南书籍的形式有效地给予消费者引导呢？正是此时，我尊敬的导师、中国侍酒师行业的驱动者——Tommy Lam 先生介绍我认识了国际酒单大奖组织。国际酒单大奖由来自澳大利亚的 Rob Hirst 先生筹办，并在澳大利亚已成功举办了 20 届，这是一个在澳大利亚乃至全球都赢得赞誉的专业酒单评选大奖。它不仅对拥有优秀酒单的餐厅予以奖项，还将这些获奖的优秀餐厅以出版的形式介绍给消费者。多年来，出任中国侍酒师大赛评委的 Rob Hirst 先生也看到了中国巨大的餐饮市场对葡萄酒的精益求精的需求。最终，在 Tommy Lam 先生筹办的侍酒师协会的协助下，"第一届中国年度酒单大奖"在 2013 年得以成功举办，并获得了非常大的反响。我很荣幸被 Rob Hirst 先生选为他的中国区合作伙伴，并共同举办了"2014 中国年度酒单大奖"。

此大奖旨在提升国内餐厅对葡萄酒酒单的重视度，也帮助我们找到国内最好的餐厅酒单。通过《中国葡萄酒餐厅指南 2014》一书，我们也将这些信息分享给更多喜爱美食美酒的消费者。

这本指南刊登了全国 23 个城市的 138 个获奖餐厅的餐品特色和酒单信息以及来自酒单大奖国际评委的专业点评。针对经常出行的商务人士，本书亦对各大国际航空公司的头等舱和商务舱的酒单做了评选，载录了拥有最佳酒单的 7 家国际航空公司名单，希望您在繁忙的旅途中也有美食和美酒的陪伴！

最后，我要非常感谢我们的出版人 Simon Fann 先生，在他的努力下，这本书才得以出版。

我们将持之以恒，每年都将呈上最新的葡萄酒餐厅名录，为您带来最好的美酒美食体验指南。

目录

2012 RESERVE & SINGLE VINEYARD RELEASE

1ST SEPTEMBER 2014

8 1/2 Otto e Mezzo 的酒窖

Mr. Gian Luca Fusetto

继香港店取得巨大成功后，米其林三星世界名厨 Umberto Bombana 又在中国大陆地区开设了首个餐厅项目——8½ Otto e Mezzo Bombana Shanghai。餐厅坐落于上海独特的地标场所洛克外滩源，并坐拥黄浦江两岸的美景。名厨 Bombana 带领充满激情的团队为食客们打造最高水平的顶级意大利美食。行政主厨 Riccardo La Perna 精选来自世界各地的食材，让客人在美食中感受意大利的美妙风光。意大利总经理兼侍酒师 Gian Luca Fusetto 亲自挑选 500 多个葡萄酒品种，为美酒爱好者创造了又一顶级的味蕾奢享。

8 ½ OTTO E MEZZO BOMBANA SHANGHAI

  最佳单一国家葡萄酒酒单

酒单大奖专家评审团之酒单点评：

一切都源于意大利——从华丽的装潢到完美的菜单和酒单。意大利精英酒商、老年份顶级酒款和众多大瓶装都是其特色。尽管酒单也会涉猎其他产区，但意大利仍是当之无愧的霸主。

A dazzling showcase of all things Italian – from the sumptuous décor to the superb menu and glittering wine list. There are feature pages for elite Italian producers, with back vintages of top wines plus a selection of magnums. While most countries are represented, the focus is undeniably Italian.

意式

¥	人均消费	RMB900
¥	葡萄酒价格	$ $ $
	酒单酒款数	500
	杯卖酒数	18
¥	杯卖酒价格	RMB90-450
¥	开 瓶 费	RMB450/ 餐厅购酒则免开瓶费
	酒单撰写人	Mr. Gian Luca Fusetto
	电 话	86 21 60872890
	营业时间	18：00-23：00
		11：00-15：00（周日早午餐）
	地 址	上海市黄浦区圆明园路协进大楼
@	网 址	www.ottoemezzobombana.com/shanghai

位于上海柏悦酒店91楼的世纪100拥有300个舒适的座位，同时提供西式、中式、日式和韩式菜肴。餐厅全部选用最新鲜的原料，每周三次从东京进口鱼类，并选用从法国、加拿大等国进口的新鲜生耗和澳大利亚的牛肉。世纪100将中、西、日、韩式菜肴集中在一本菜单里，其中包括海鲜类、寿司、烧烤、炉烧、清蒸和清炒。客人还可以根据心情随意选择用餐的区域，包括由胡桃木做成的船舱椅、熟食区的酒吧椅、寿司吧的柜台椅，同时还有可以容纳6到16人的4间包房。

100 CENTURY AVENUE
世纪 100

酒单大奖专家评审团之酒单点评：

从颜色分类，再到葡萄品种、国家及地区，这个酒单全面展示了世界各地的酒款。酒单完全由高品质酒款组成，其中不乏有机或生物动力法的酒款。由多达35余款杯卖酒组成的酒单让人眼前一亮。

This list celebrates the diversity of the world of wine, with wines arranged by colour, then variety, country and region. Quality is high across the board, with attention paid to the inclusion of sustainably produced wine. The by-the-glass offering is stunning, with over 35 wines available.

西式、中式

¥	人均消费	RMB500-600
¥	葡萄酒价格	$ $ $
	酒单酒款数	500
	杯卖酒数	36
¥	杯卖酒价格	RMB110-480
	酒单撰写人	Mr. Adrian Zhang & Mr. Jean-Marc Nolant
	电　话	86 21 68881234
	营业时间	11：30 - 14:30, 17：30 - 22:30
	地　址	上海市浦东陆家嘴世纪大道 100 号柏悦酒店 91 楼
@	网　址	www.shanghai.park.hyatt.com

布迪格乐是中国首家"100% 波尔多"概念的葡萄酒餐厅，并受到波尔多葡萄酒行业协会 (CIVB) 倾力支持。餐厅不仅允许消费者在店内享用葡萄酒，而且对外零售波尔多葡萄酒，旨在为中国美酒爱好者呈现"优雅、平衡、多元化"的波尔多葡萄酒享受。除了精选的波尔多葡萄酒，布迪格乐还带来了诸多法国特色的经典餐食，带给中国消费者全方位的波尔多美酒体验。

BURDIGALA
布迪格乐葡萄酒餐厅

法式

酒单大奖专家评审团之酒单点评：

在中国，波尔多的价格经常超过顾客预算，但是值得高兴的是，这间现代法国小酒馆推出一些价格合理、不太出名的产区和风格的酒款。当然，这里也不会少了名庄。参观隔壁的专卖店也是旅程中的一站。

Bordeaux in China is often priced beyond the reach of the average wine lover. So it's refreshing to see this modern French bistro promoting some affordable, lesser-known appellations and styles, as well as respected grand cru classes. A visit to the adjoining wine store is a must.

¥	人均消费：	RMB160
¥	葡萄酒价格：	$ $
	酒单酒款数：	70
	杯卖酒款数：	7
¥	杯卖酒价格：	RMB45-65
¥	开 瓶 费：	RMB250
	酒单撰写人：	Mr. Franck Boudot
	电 话：	86 21 64229826
	营业时间：	11：30 - 24：00
	地 址：	上海市徐汇区嘉善路 301 号 2 楼
@	网 址：	www.theburdigala.com

凯旋的时尚氛围及上乘的国际餐饮专为迎合来往于世界各地、懂得欣赏不同美食的旅客。凯旋内设多种餐饮处所，包括餐厅、酒廊、露天餐厅及马提尼酒吧，为处于时尚环境之中的宾客带来一系列各具特色的餐饮体验。

CACHET - ALL DAY DINING
凯旋餐厅

国际

酒单大奖专家评审团之酒单点评：

酒款的数量几乎是去年的两倍之多，但令人欣喜的是，高质量的世界知名酒款仍然处在核心地位。诸如 JJP、Felton Road、Peter Lehmann 和 Duval—Leroy 一类的酒款一直都备受欢迎。若想找到明星酒款，那就去看看顶级酒水单部分吧。

This list has almost doubled from last year but it's good to see its strong inner core of world class wines from the most reliable names in the business remains. Names like J.J.Prum, Felton Road, Peter Lehmann and Duval-Leroy are always welcome. Pop into the Premium Cellar list for star finds.

¥	人均消费：	RMB300
¥	葡萄酒价格：	$ $
♉	酒单酒款数：	69
♉	杯卖酒款数：	11
♟	酒单撰写人：	Mr. Michael Zhang
☎	电　　话：	86 21 23302288
⏰	营业时间：	6：30 - 23：30
⌂	地　　址：	上海市卢湾区马当路99号
		新天地朗廷酒店1楼
@	网　　址：	www.xintiandi.langhamhotels.com

Calypso 地中海餐厅为食客们提供纯正意大利及地中海风味美食，包括来自海陆的各色食材、样式繁多的共享式开胃菜以及午市简餐套餐。正宗那不勒斯披萨、意大利芝士、自制意面和冰淇淋等多款美食正等待着您悦动的味蕾。独立的楼梯直通二楼宽敞的露天酒廊，款款美酒与浓厚的现代风情融会贯通，为您呈现沪上最摩登的精致酒廊。

CALYPSO RESTAURANT & LOUNGE
CALYPSO 地中海餐厅

地中海式

酒单大奖专家评审团之酒单点评：

这份现代酒单与餐厅明亮轻快的地中海菜单相协调。白葡萄酒是以花香、果香或矿物感来排序，而红葡萄酒则是根据品种来分类。酒单包罗万象，酒品价格合理，还不乏极特别的酒款。

This modern list is in step with the restaurant's bright, airy surrounds and contemporary Mediterranean menu. Whites are classified in the flower, fruit or mineral spectrum while reds are organised varietally. There's a kaleidoscope of well-priced wines from around the globe plus the odd icon.

人均消费：RMB300
葡萄酒价格：$ $
酒单酒款数：110
杯卖酒数：19
杯卖酒价格：RMB70-120
酒单撰写人：Mr. Jerry Liao
电　　话：86 21 22036570
营业时间：11：00 - 23：00
地　　址：上海市铜仁路近安义路静安嘉里中心南区广场
网　　址：www.calypsoshanghai.com

Miss Ying Guo

东西荟萃的时尚餐厅 Camelia 提供现代法式佳肴。精英厨师团队来自巴黎乔治五世的米其林餐厅。别具一格的户外露台和室内酒廊都是餐后小酌的上佳选择。侍酒师郭莹获本年度"世界最佳青年侍酒师"之一的荣誉。她的美酒推荐将令宾客得到完美的饕餮之宴。

CAMELIA

最佳酒店餐厅酒单
最佳开胃酒酒单
最佳餐后酒酒单
2014 中国酒单大奖 – 决赛入围名单

法式

酒单大奖专家评审团之酒单点评：

只要瞄上一眼，您就会知道酒单撰写人的水平之高。侍酒师郭莹为您带来一份精彩绝伦的酒单。不论是知名酒庄还是精品酒庄，个个都是明星级别。产区被严格地划分开，旨在给您带来真正意义上全球化的体验。

A mere glimpse is all that's needed to see there's an expert at the helm. Sommelier Ying Guo presents an inspirational list, full of the brightest stars of the wine world – from famous icons to boutique gems. Regionality is taken seriously to ensure a true global experience is offered.

人均消费：	RMB300
葡萄酒价格：	$ $ $
酒单酒款数：	260
杯卖酒数：	16
杯卖酒价格：	RMB90-190
酒单撰写人：	Miss Ying Guo
电　话：	86 21 20361300
营业时间：	全天
地　址：	上海市浦东新区世纪大道 210 号 浦东四季酒店 1 楼
网　址：	www.fourseasons.com/pudong

华懋阁西餐厅荟萃欧式顶级美食，宾客可一边俯瞰外滩的优美景致，一边品尝雅致的欧陆式时尚家常菜。20 世纪 30 年代以来，华懋阁即成为和平饭店创始人沙逊爵士和其他游走世界的富绅们享用美味的地方。国际政要、名人名流都聚集于此。如今，您亦可以在精致华丽、酒香四溢的宜人氛围中尽情享受主厨精心烹制的绝佳菜肴，细细品味 200 多款精选的欧美顶级佳酿。此外，崭新的开放式露台是餐前酒后的最佳去处，华懋阁还提供特色鸡尾酒及欧式小食，您可在享用饕餮美食的同时，以 360°的视角欣赏到浦江两岸的天际线。

CATHAY ROOM
华懋阁

欧式

酒单大奖专家评审团之酒单点评：

这是一份充满现代欧洲风格的酒单，它囊括了让人倍感可信又熟悉的酒款。杯卖酒款的可选择范围和优质中国葡萄酒的入选更是为其增添光彩。当然，老年份的酒款也是其亮点之一。

A contemporary European-flavoured wine list that stars a strong selection of the ever reliable and the familiar. The wines by the glass listing and the presence of a goodly number of Chinese wines to be applauded. Older vintages are also a feature.

💴	人均消费	RMB500
💴	葡萄酒价格：	$ $ $
🍷	酒单酒款数：	250
🍷	杯卖酒数：	20
💴	杯卖酒价格：	RMB69-229
💴	开 瓶 费	禁止外带酒水
👤	酒单撰写人：	Mr. Eddy Shi
📞	电 话	86 21 61386881
🕐	营业时间：	12：00-14：30，18：00-22：30
🏠	地 址：	上海市黄浦区南京东路20 号和平饭店
@	网 址：	www.fairmont.com/peace-hotel-shanghai

作为一家现代牛扒餐厅与酒吧，"恰"专注于高品质食材、简单粗犷的菜肴口味以及充满趣味的呈现方式，为往来饕客带来奢华又清新随意的美食体验。目前"恰"是全上海唯一一家提供顶级澳大利亚 Blackmore 和牛柳的餐厅。为了增加在餐厅用餐的独特魅力，"恰"从全球引进一系列手工制造的牛排刀组合，让客人们能在用餐时自由选择心仪的刀具。同时，"恰"特别提供六种精选天然海盐，完美搭配餐厅的各种美食。

CHAR BAR & GRILL
恰餐厅酒吧

酒单大奖专家评审团之酒单点评：

中肯的菜单和酒单使其成为深受当地人和游客喜爱的地方，更不要说它漂亮的景色了。以风格作分类的酒单便顾客挑选，同时涉猎了来自法国、澳大利亚等众多国家的酒款，另外还有 15 款杯卖酒。

The honesty of both the menu and wine list makes this an endearing favourite of locals and visitors alike, not to mention the stunning views. Wines are grouped by style to make selection easier, with a fair spread from France and Australia. 15 by the glass.

牛排馆

- 💰 人均消费：RMB550
- 💰 葡萄酒价格：$ $
- 🍷 酒单酒款数：100
- 🍷 杯卖酒数：15
- 💰 杯卖酒价格：RMB90-160
- 💰 开瓶费：RMB300
- 👤 酒单撰写人：Mr. Barthélémy Lee
- 📞 电　话：86 21 33029995
- 🕐 营业时间：18：00 - 22：30
- 🏠 地　址：上海市黄浦区中山东二路 585 号
  外滩英迪格酒店顶层
- @ 网　址：www.char-thebund.com

雍福会主要供应复古传统的上海佳肴，钻研汇整本帮地道口味，提供精准的西式服务。在这里，你可以惬意地重拾十里洋场的典雅生活品位。"经典、古典、传菜"都是雍福会的"吃"文化。而雍福会所提供的地道"本帮传菜"也讲究时令概念，选用最佳时节的蟹、野生的河虾以及又大又肥美的长江回鱼，以追求其原汁原味的神韵。

YONG FOO ELITE
雍福会

最佳俱乐部酒单

上海菜式

酒单大奖专家评审团之酒单点评：

法国酒在酒单上占主导地位，尤其是顶级勃艮第和波尔多酒。如果你想从左岸或者夜丘明星庄里跳脱出来，那么还有大把的西班牙酒、意大利酒和澳大利亚酒供你选择。红葡萄酒是本酒单的亮点。

French wines dominate the list, particularly top end Burgundy and Bordeaux. Though if looking for something other than a left bank icon or a Cote de Nuits star, then there are a handful of Spanish, Italian and Australian wines worth a look. The red selection trumps the whites.

¥	人均消费：	RMB500-1000
¥	葡萄酒价格：	$ $ $
🍷	酒单酒款数：	116
♟	杯卖酒款数：	8
¥	杯卖酒价格：	RMB60-190
¥	开瓶费：	非会员收取
✍	酒单撰写人：	Mr. Ian Dai
📞	电　话：	86 21 54662727
🕙	营业时间：	11：30 - 00：00
🏠	地　址：	上海市徐汇区永福路 200 号
@	网　址：	www.yongfooelite.com

上海浦东文华东方酒店的现代派法式餐厅——58°扒房由才华横溢并屡获国际殊荣的顶级名厨 Richard Ekkebus 领军。优选上等新鲜食材，配以绝伦的烹制技艺，58°扒房聚焦法国传统餐饮的精髓，为宾客奉上极致的法国馥逸浪漫美食。58°扒房位于酒店一层，与室外贯通，为客人提供露天花园餐桌。整个餐厅洋溢着 20 世纪二三十年代上海滩装饰艺术的氛围。法式开放厨房精心为宾客献上手工鲜切熟食、炭火干炙熏肉及鲜焙香酵法包，同时，宾客还将享受到充满法式风情的各式餐点，并从列有250 余种酒饮的酒水单中挑选心爱的酒品，尽享心仪之选。

FIFTY 8° GRILL
58° 扒房

酒单大奖专家评审团之酒单点评：

法国爱好者对这里的法国美食和优雅的环境一定赞不绝口。酒单也着眼于经典款——大量的香槟、勃艮第和波尔多。除此之外，罗讷河谷和物美价廉的南部酒也可以一试。这是一份选择均衡的酒单。

Francophiles will delight in the fine French food and the refined surrounds. The wine list focuses on the classics – plenty of Champagne, Burgundy and Bordeaux – you'll also find some lovely Rhones plus some affordable picks from the south. Balanced international selection.

法式

¥	人均消费	RMB490
¥	葡萄酒价格	$ $ $
🍷	酒单酒款数	311
♟	杯卖酒款数	18
¥	杯卖酒价格	RMB95-190
🙎	酒单撰写人	Mr. Stephane Buliard
☎	电　话	86 21 20829938
⏱	营业时间	11：30 - 14：30，17：30 - 22：30
🏠	地　　址	上海市浦东新区浦东南路 111 号 文华东方酒店行政公寓大堂 1 层
@	网　　址	www.mandarinoriental.com/shanghai

这里是魅力与高雅的所在，这里弥漫着神秘与迷人的气氛，时髦的、舒适的、个性的、随性的、性感的、火辣的都在这里融合。这里拥有 3 个魅力别致的吧台，精美可口的美食。从小吃到盛宴，一应俱全，更有迷人奢华的浪漫氛围、无与伦比的外滩美景、各种派对以及 DJ 电音，让消费者度过一个舒适愉快的浪漫时光。红酒吧拥有 32 种以杯出售和 36 种以瓶出售的品牌红酒；令人震慑的性感香槟吧提供 5 种以杯出售的品牌香槟，更有可供选择的丰富酒单；当然，标志性的鸡尾酒吧还供应魅力的经典饮品，推出独特的创新酒单。

GLAMOUR BAR
魅力酒吧

酒吧

酒单大奖专家评审团之酒单点评：

在这家别致又时髦的上海酒吧里，你能找到许多心头好。知名酒款的跨度很大，包括用杯卖机出售的 32 款杯卖酒和带有异域风情名称的鸡尾酒。在香槟吧，啜口法国汽泡，咬着软壳蟹棒，这是何等的享受！

Plenty to like at this chic and sassy Shanghai bar. An international spread of well-known wines, including 32 by-the-glass via an Enoteca, plus an enticing array of exotically named cocktails. Sip fine French fizz at the Champagne bar while snacking on soft shell crab buns and other fancy bites.

¥	人均消费	RMB128
¥	葡萄酒价格	$ $
	酒单酒款数	68
¥	杯卖酒数	32
¥	杯卖酒价格	RMB68-199
¥	开瓶费	RMB200
	酒单撰写人	Mr. Zi Zheng Xu
	电　话	86 21 63509988
	营业时间	17：00 - 午夜
	地　　址	上海市黄浦区中山东一路 5 号 6 楼
@	网　址	www.m-glamour.com/home.html

屡获殊荣的"桂花楼"中餐厅主营地道的淮扬菜、粤菜、本帮菜及川菜。宾客可以在时尚现代与中国传统元素结合的环境中享用美味佳肴。

GUI HUA LOU
桂花楼

  最佳美食和美酒搭配酒单

酒单大奖专家评审团之酒单点评：

富豪们可以随意选瓶 DRC 或者波尔多列级庄来配餐。我们则可以在为数不少且享有国际声誉的酒款中挑选一番。众多适合佐餐的酒款都可搭配淮扬菜、上海菜和四川菜。

High-rollers are catered for with a spread of Romanee-Contis and classified Bordeauxs. For the rest of us, there's a moderate number of carefully selected wines with international reupte. Plenty of food friendly options to match the refined Huaiyangnese, Shanghainese and Sichuanese menu.

中式

人均消费：	RMB260
葡萄酒价格：	$ $ $
杯卖酒数：	6
杯卖酒价格：	RMB78-138
酒单撰写人：	Mr. Neil Zhu
电　话：	86 21 68828888
营业时间：	11：30-15：00, 17：30-22：00
地　　址：	上海市浦东新区富城路 33 号
网　　址：	www.shangri-la.com

Henkes 位于追求高端品质的芮欧百货内。餐厅设有大型的户外花园，宾客可以在舒适的环境里，享用美食、呼吸静安公园的新鲜空气。餐厅位于地铁静安寺站的正上方，交通便捷。一定不要错过 Henkes 的美味自创菜品：自制的烟熏三文鱼配上新鲜的茴香根，柠檬汁，水瓜榴；辣味烤鸡；澳大利亚肉眼牛扒；咸味冰激凌、巧克力慕斯等特有甜品。

HENKES

最佳中型酒单

地中海式

酒单大奖专家评审团之酒单点评：

这份简洁且平衡的酒单与地中海菜系交相呼应，让人一窥葡萄酒世界的究竟。著名酒商的佳作和价格亲民的酒款并存。这里既有被细心挑选出来的白葡萄酒，也有深度较广的红葡萄酒，其中不乏老年份酒款。

A succinct, well-balanced list, that's complementary to the Mediterranean menu, which offers diners a snapshot of the world of wine. Respected producers sit alongside lesser-known affordable drops. There's a careful selection of whites and a more extensive range of reds many with age.

¥	人均消费：	RMB200
¥	葡萄酒价格：	$ $
🍷	酒单酒款数：	83
🍷	杯卖酒款数：	9
¥	杯卖酒价格：	RMB50-145
¥	开瓶费：	RMB250
👤	酒单撰写人：	Mr. Max Haahr
📞	电　　话：	86 21 32530889
🕐	营业时间：	10：00-23：00
🏠	地　　址：	上海市静安区南京西路 1601 号 芮欧百货 1 楼 1E 室
@	网　　址：	www.henkes.com.cn

备受赞誉的翡翠 36 餐厅曾荣获各种奖项，如"中国 10 佳商务餐厅"、《亚洲最佳餐厅指南》评选的
"亚洲最好餐厅"之一、"*Tatler*"杂志评选的"上海最好的餐厅"之一，同时翡翠 36 餐厅还喜获《餐厅》杂志"2013 亚洲最佳 50 餐厅"称号。宾客可以一边欣赏旖旎的外滩风光，一边品尝各种精致的美味佳肴。翡翠 36 餐厅特别推出周日早午餐，为客人们奉上周日味觉盛宴。

JADE ON 36 RESTAURANT
翡翠 36 餐厅

酒单大奖专家评审团之酒单点评：

也许波尔多一级庄的老年份、摩泽尔的 JJP、阿尔萨斯车库酒 Meyer-Fonne 才让这份酒单这样地出彩，亮点太多却难以抉择。这是一份荟萃世界顶级酒款的酒单。

It could be the back-vintage runs of First Growth Bordeaux, or simple additions like Mosel's amazing JJ Prum and cult producer Meyer-Fonne from Alsace, but this list is so dazzling with stars it's hard to decide where to drink. A prestige list of some of the world's great wines here.

法式

¥	人均消费	RMB1000
❤	葡萄酒价格	$ $ $
🍸	酒单酒款数	450
🍷	杯卖酒款数	17
👤	酒单撰写人	Mr. Henry Zhou
☎	电　话	86 21 68828888-280
🕐	营业时间	18：00 - 02：30
		11：30 - 15：00(周日早午餐)
🏠	地　址	上海市浦东新区富城路 33 号
		紫金楼 36 层
@	网　址	www.shangri-la.com

这里有别致的装潢、热情周到的服务以及正宗的传统粤菜。主要用餐区可容纳 52 位客人，6 间私人雅间可容纳 64 位客人，2 间贵宾包间可容纳 40 位客人。行政主厨黄英杰师傅携团队选用品质上乘的新鲜食材，以全新的方式，为食客献上多重感官的地道粤式盛筵。

JIN XUAN CHINESE RESTAURANT
金轩

酒单大奖专家评审团之酒单点评：

奢华的装修、极好的粤菜和全球精选葡萄酒给你带来超五星的用餐体验。酒单的覆盖面广，尤其列有多种意大利酒款和张弛有度的波尔多酒。新世界酒款也很好地被罗列其中。

The triumvirate of lavish décor, a spectacular Cantonese menu and a truly global wine list makes for a top notch dining experience. The wine list spans the globe, with a surprisingly extensive Italian collection and a healthy spread of Bordeaux's. The new world is well represented.

粤式

人均消费：RMB600-800
葡萄酒价格：$ $ $
酒单酒款数：425
杯卖酒数：16
杯卖酒价格：RMB95-360
开 瓶 费：RMB300
酒单撰写人：Mr. Henry Ng
电　　话：86 21 20201768
营业时间：11：30 - 14：00，17：30 - 22：00
地　　址：上海市浦东陆家嘴世纪大道 8 号浦东丽思卡尔顿酒店 53 楼
网　　址：www.ritzcarlton.com

静安餐厅位于璞丽酒店二楼，备有 120 个座位，客人在此可尽赏静安公园的如茵美景。行政总厨 Michael Wilson 擅长将传统与创新相结合，融合自身的热诚和投入，为宾客呈现全新味蕾享受。餐厅始终坚持选用上好的新鲜食材，通过中西合璧的烹调方法以及时令食材的不同搭配，追求每道菜的极致奢华口感。

JING'AN RESTAURANT
静安餐厅

欧陆式

酒单大奖专家评审团之酒单点评：

不同寻常的酒单与反传统的菜色的完美搭配。当然，你会找到顶级香槟、波尔多贵族和一系列全球知名酒款，还有 24 款杯卖酒和新奇的酒商。过于独特的酒款可以退役了，但是其他部分还是非常不错的。

The eccentric note to this list matches the unconventional flavour combinations found in the menu. Sure, you'll find swish Champagnes, blue-blood Bordeaux and a swathe of global names. But also 24 wines-by-glass and some quirky producers. The odd wine need retiring but otherwise its great.

¥	人均消费	RMB230-500
¥	葡萄酒价格	$ $ $
♠♣	酒单酒款数	327
♟	杯卖酒数	28
¥	杯卖酒价格	RMB85-230
¥	开 瓶 费	RMB300
♟	酒单撰写人	Ms. Fion Wong
☎	电 话	86 21 22166988
⏰	营业时间	06：30 - 22：00
⌂	地 址	上海市静安区常德路 1 号
@	网 址	www.jinganrestaurant.com

卡卡图是位于澳大利亚北部的著名天然野生动植物区。它拥有壮丽的景观、富饶的物产和最原始的土著文化。成立于 2007 年的上海 "卡卡图"给中国带来了具有现代感的澳大利亚美食。餐厅通过选用澳大利亚鳄鱼、鸵鸟以及卡卡图当地最著名的肺鱼，制作出富有创意和令人兴奋的菜单，同时提供澳洲高品质的葡萄酒和特色鸡尾酒。卡卡图的装饰墙画均是澳大利亚各原始部落的艺术品，同时，特色鱼缸能让宾客轻松感受到异域的环境。

KAKADU
卡卡图

澳大利亚式

酒单大奖专家评审团之酒单点评：

这个澳洲餐吧提供众多酒款，尽管你还需要去其糟粕取其精华。很高兴在这里找到克莱谷雷司令和猎人谷赛美容，还有众多产区的霞多丽、饱满多汁的红酒和优质的黑皮诺，这其中也包括一些新西兰经典酒。

Plenty of options at this Aussie restaurant and bar though you'll need to sift through the sand to find the jewels. Nice to see classic Clare Valley rieslings and Hunter semillons, along with the diverse regional spread of chardonnays, juicy reds and quality pinots, including some kiwi classics.

¥	人均消费：	RMB190
¥	葡萄酒价格：	$ $
▼	杯卖酒数：	11
¥	杯卖酒价格：	RMB45-70
¥	开瓶费：	RMB200
♟	酒单撰写人：	Mr. James Sing
☏	电　　话：	86 21 54680118
◷	营业时间：	09：30 - 12：30
⌂	地　　址：	上海市建国中路 1104A 室
@	网　　址：	www.facebook.com/kakadushanghaichina. com

Kartel 是一座三层楼的豪华酒吧，位于前上海法租界的核心地段。酒吧一共有三层，两层室内以及一层屋顶露台，六楼空中法式花园，顶楼露台 360°景色无遮挡，是户外饮酒、赏景、享晚餐的最佳小憩的地方。五楼用木质地板、裸露的砖墙和黑板菜单进行装饰，一个玻璃封闭的酒架延伸至整面墙，巧妙地将酒单和温馨气氛组合起来。Kartel 的菜肴大多设计得很适合分享，比如 tapas 小食、樱桃番茄马苏里拉奶酪。享用一锅勃艮第牛肉，抑或是一盘巴斯克鸡肉，悠闲地品尝葡萄酒，或是一杯艳丽的鸡尾酒。

KARTEL

酒吧

酒单大奖专家评审团之酒单点评：

这个品位不错的酒吧有很多法国酒，从性价比高的朗格多克－鲁西荣和卢瓦河谷，到经典的红葡萄酒和优质香槟。至于"全球"这个概念，从一系列简单易饮的酒款中，你可窥其端倪。

There a strong French focus at this classy bar, including affordable wines from the appellations of the Languedoc-Rousillon and Loire Valley, plus a few 'classic' reds and fine champagnes. As for the 'world wines', there's a succinct selection of quaffable drops.

¥	人均消费	RMB130
¥	葡萄酒价格	$
	酒单酒款数	200
	杯卖酒数	100
	酒单撰写人	Mr. Louis Lu
	电　话	86 21 54042899
	营业时间	18：00 - 01：00
	地　址	上海市襄阳北路 1 号 5 楼
@	网　址	www.kartel.com.cn

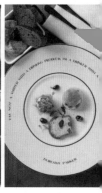

这里是集书店、餐厅、酒吧、印刷空间和画廊为一体，由新华传媒荣誉出品的生活体验空间。以光比喻艺术文化，以盐比喻美食佳酿，"光与盐"拥有一系列独具特色的店面及品牌，将为最具鉴赏力的客人带来崭新体验。其旗下的 Ms. Ding Dining 是一家经典海派西餐厅，呈现的菜品令人联想起 20 世纪 30 年代上海老式西餐的格调。餐厅的名字是为了纪念丁淑静女士——基督教女青年会在中国的创始人而起。同时，在 Ms. Ding Dining 餐厅中的 Mei Ling´s Room 更是为了纪念曾在此工作过的宋美龄女士而设。

LIGHT & SALT
光与盐

老克拉海派创意菜

酒单大奖专家评审团之酒单点评：

让我们回到 20 世纪 30 年代的上海，在 Miss Dings Dining 喝杯小酒或者是在 Library Distillery 来杯餐后酒。这份酒单具有现代风格，以葡萄品种作分类，有合理的价格和优质的酒商。红葡萄酒部分的实力很强劲。

Step back in time to 1930s Shanghai and drink fine wine in Miss Dings Dining room followed by an extensive range of digestives in the Library Distillery. The wine list has a contemporary edge, with varietal groupings, realistic prices and quality producers – the red section is particularly strong.

¥	人均消费：	RMB300
¥	葡萄酒价格：	$ $
🍷	酒单酒款数：	95
🍷	杯卖酒数：	16
¥	杯卖酒价格：	RMB65-150
👤	酒单撰写人：	Mr. Brandon Ho
📞	电　　话：	86 21 63611086
🏠	地　　址：	上海市黄浦区圆明园路 133 号
		（女青年会大楼）6 楼
@	网　　址：	www.light-n-salt.com

Miss Melanie Canou

独具异域风情的鸡尾酒、甘醇馥郁的香槟和葡萄酒、口味纯正的咖啡和茗茶，在美丽幽静的内湖、瀑布和繁茂的植物环绕中，令消费者心旷神怡，悠然忘我。

LINK LOUNGE

大堂吧

酒单大奖专家评审团之酒单点评：

作为大堂吧的酒单来说，这是不容忽视的存在。超过30款杯卖酒，包括4款香槟和一些基本酒款的组合。如果认真研读这份酒单，你就能发现许多受人尊敬的酒商，比如 Jaboulet、Craggy Range 和 Alain Chabanon。偶像酒款首当其冲。

An extensive list for a lobby bar. Over 30 wines by the glass, including 4 Champagnes, and a couple of basic wine flights – overall a good global spread. Study the list closely to discover some respected producers such as Jaboulet , Craggy Range and Alain Chabanon. Icons listed up front.

¥	人均消费：	RMB120
¥	葡萄酒价格：	$ $ $
	酒单酒款数：	106
¥	杯卖酒数：	28
¥	杯卖酒价格：	RMB58-258
¥	开瓶费：	RMB200
	酒单撰写人：	Miss Melanie Canou
	电　话：	86 21 37611909
	营业时间：	08：30 - 22：30
	地　址：	上海东方佘山索菲特大酒店 主楼二层大堂
@	网　址：	www.sofitel.com

最地道的意大利风味美食——小母牛肉、经典面食和创新菜式——金枪鱼鞑靼和罕见的烹煮三文鱼都来到了上海。家庭风味的烹饪与餐厅氛围融为一体，这家现代的意大利餐厅位于卢湾区并靠近新天地。在这里就餐就像在朋友家吃饭一样——拥有较为随意的风格和美味的食物。这家位于邻里间的餐厅值得一试。

LUCCIO'S

最佳精致酒单

意式

酒单大奖专家评审团之酒单点评：

这个邻家小馆的酒单拥有众多可以尝试而且售价合理的酒款。餐厅自行进口的酒款则出现在私人精选的法国和意大利酒部分。酒单虽短，半数则能杯卖，而且每款都带有酒评及配餐建议。

Plenty to like at this neighbourhood eatery where wine can be enjoyed without breaking the bank. There's a personal selection of French and Italian wines, imported by the restaurant. Though the list is small, over half are available by the glass and there are helpful tasting notes for each wine.

¥	人均消费	RMB150
¥	葡萄酒价格	$ $
	酒单酒款数	50
	杯卖酒数	20
¥	杯卖酒价格	RMB37-108
¥	开瓶费	购买一瓶则免一瓶开瓶费
	酒单撰写人	Mr. Paul Hopkins
	电 话	86 21 53520587
	营业时间	11：00 - 23：00
	地 址	上海市淡水路 242 号
@	网 址	www.luccios.com.cn

米氏西餐厅位于黄浦江畔外滩的一幢7层大厦的顶楼，老板 Michelle Garnaut 的设计团队赋予了这幢始建于 1927 年的原日清船运大楼以全新的想象。餐厅在风格上融合了旧上海的风情与 21 世纪的现代设计元素。餐厅内设有可容纳 120 坐席的主餐室以及极富魅力的水晶餐室。如置身其中，巍然壮观的外滩景色尽收眼底，或者宾客站在露台上俯瞰黄浦江与对岸的滨江美景。

M ON THE BUND
米氏西餐厅

  2014 中国酒单大奖 – 决赛入围名单

酒单大奖专家评审团之酒单点评：

这是一份价格合理、富有个性而且亲民的酒单。它分成精简版和完整版——同时满足日常用餐和葡萄酒爱好者的需求。酒单上的全球顶级生产商既有进步卓越的，也有金字塔顶端的。中国葡萄酒的入选让人眼前一亮。

Sensible, different and free of pretense - it's divided into a short and long list – catering for the regular fine-diner and wine buff simultaneously. Top international producers are in abundance, with quality rising to the highest levels. Also refreshing to see a decent number of Chinese wines.

现代欧式

¥	人均消费：	RMB398
¥	葡萄酒价格：	$ $ $
🍷	酒单酒款数：	300
🍷	杯卖酒数：	32
¥	杯卖酒价格：	RMB60-140
¥	开瓶费：	RMB200
👤	酒单撰写人：	Mr. Zi Zheng Xu
☎	电　话：	86 21 63509988
🕐	营业时间：	11：30-14：30（周一至周五）；
		11：30-17：00（周末）;18：00-22：30
🏠	地　址：	上海市黄浦区中山东一路5号7楼
@	网　址：	www.m-restaurantgroup.com/mbund

Maya 有很多值得一试的招牌菜肴，像传统的墨西哥塔可饼、玉米饼和酸橘汁腌制海鲜；创意的馄饨脆皮鱼塔可和芝士南瓜辣椒；主打的烤阿根廷牛排配土豆和煎海鲈鱼配椰味甜薯。鸡尾酒单和红酒单更能体现出专业的 Maya 精神。精选的鸡尾酒融合了传统与经典，极具风味异国情调元素。红酒单更包括了北美、南美、西欧、东欧等新兴产地的珍酿。

MAYA MEXICAN RESTAURANT & BAR
玛雅餐厅

墨西哥式

酒单大奖专家评审团之酒单点评：

这份平易近人的酒单以风格作分类。杯卖酒款涉及多种葡萄品种，价格也很合理。多数国家和葡萄品种都有涉猎——性价比不错的西班牙酒也在选择范围中。这份酒单就像万花筒一样，五彩缤纷。

A vibrant, friendly, approachable list with wines grouped by style. Prices are accessible and there's a good varietal spread by the glass. Most major countries and varieties are represented – including a solid selection of Spanish wines. Its like a mixed bag of lollies for grown ups.

¥	人均消费：	RMB250
¥	葡萄酒价格：	$
▮▯	酒单酒款数：	85
▮	杯卖酒数：	11
¥	杯卖酒价格：	RMB48-68
♋	酒单撰写人：	Mr. Rob Jameson
☎	电　　话：	86 21 62896889
⏱	营业时间：	17：00 - 深夜（周一至周五）；
		11：00 - 深夜（周末）
⌂	地　　址：	上海市静安区巨鹿路 568 弄
		四方新城俱乐部 2 楼
@	网　　址：	www.cosmogroup.cn

上海莫尔顿牛排坊乃世界最大的莫尔顿餐厅，拥有400个座位。餐厅亦设有9间包房，配备先进的视听设备，并为雪茄和葡萄酒行家特设2间贵宾房。阳台可供举办私人露天晚宴和鸡尾酒会，客人在此可以欣赏东方明珠电视塔以及浦东壮美的都市胜景。莫尔顿牛排坊提供顶级谷物喂养而成的牛的牛肉、新鲜鱼类、波士顿大龙虾、羊排、鸡肉等美食。餐厅提供的牛排份量足，包括48盎司（1300克）的上等腰肉牛排、20盎司（550克）的顶级纽约西冷牛排和12盎司（340克）的双份特厚牛柳。

MORTON'S THE STEAKHOUSE SHANGHAI
莫尔顿牛排坊 – 上海

酒单大奖专家评审团之酒单点评：

这是莫尔顿牛排坊在上海的分店，酒款与北京店类似，均以搭配牛排的美国酒为主，另有50种酒款。这里有更多可供选择的大瓶装和波尔多红葡萄酒，对于消费者而言，这无疑是件好事，不是吗？

A sister restaurant to Morton's Steak House in Beijing with a similar wine list featuring American wines to suit the steak house setting but with nearly 50 extra wines. Here, there are more magnums and more Bordeaux reds to choose from which isn't a bad thing at all.

美式

¥	人均消费	RMB800-1000
¥	葡萄酒价格	$ $
🍶	酒单酒款数	300
🍷	杯卖酒数	24
¥	杯卖酒价格	RMB118-254
👤	酒单撰写人	Mr. Royce Ye
📞	电　话	86 21 60758888
🕐	营业时间	11：30 - 23：00
🏠	地　址	上海市浦东陆家嘴世纪大道8号国金中心商场4楼15-16号商铺
@	网　址	www.mortons.com

莫尔顿海鲜牛排坊标志着莫尔顿在中国的全新概念。餐厅不仅提供享誉世界的招牌美食——最上乘的顶级进口熟成谷饲牛排，更推出顶级海鲜美食。8米长的海鲜吧台陈列着每日从美国、法国、澳大利亚及新西兰新鲜运抵上海滩的海鲜食材，包括9种新鲜生蚝。餐厅菜单上的海鲜品种丰富，极具亚洲特色，份大量足。餐厅延续莫尔顿一如既往的风格，提供众多美味配菜、奢华丰盛的甜点以及顶级葡萄酒、烈酒和鸡尾酒等丰富多彩的佳酿。

Mr. Diego Zhang

MORTON'S STEAK AND SEAFOOD GRILLE SHANGHAI
莫尔顿海鲜牛排坊 – 上海

美式

酒单大奖专家评审团之酒单点评：

这是一份既囊括顶级酒款又兼顾了可搭配铁板牛排和海鲜酒款的酒单。红葡萄酒包括了美国主流葡萄品种的佳酿，意大利、澳大利亚和阿根廷也不落后，反而法国酒不是主流。杯卖酒也有亮点。

A balanced list with plenty of top wines to complement sizzled steak and seafood. Reds are up first, with a solid selection of American beauties across all main varieties. Assertive reds from Italy, Australia and Argentina are a feature, less so those from France. Some lovely wines by-the-glass.

¥	人均消费：	RMB600-800
¥	葡萄酒价格：	$ $
♟	酒单酒款数：	180
♟	杯卖酒款数：	22
¥	杯卖酒价格：	RMB79-284
☻	酒单撰写人：	Mr. Diego Zhang
✆	电　话：	86 21 60677888
◷	营业时间：	11：30 - 24：00
⌂	地　址：	上海市徐汇区淮海中路 999 号环贸 iapm 商场 4 楼
@	网　址：	www.mortons.com/shanghaigrille

Mr. Willis 是一家意式简餐店，供应正宗的比萨。餐厅的装修具有北欧的简约风格，室外采用和室内一样的地板。同时，餐厅内置很多鲜花、小雏菊、百合、太阳花、绣球花、仙人球、迷迭香等，配着烛光，带来温馨浪漫的用餐氛围。

MR. WILLIS

意式

酒单大奖专家评审团之酒单点评：

啜上一口精选的葡萄酒，这舒适的用餐氛围是如此让人沉醉。这家餐厅自行进口的许多新鲜有趣的酒款等待你去发掘。毫无疑问，这是一份有着西班牙、意大利、法国、澳大利亚和新西兰酒款的精致酒单。

Soak up the convivial ambience of this modern eatery while sipping on one of the carefully selected wines. The restaurant has specially imported many of the labels so you will find some new and different wines to enjoy. Decent selections from Spain, Italy, France, Australia and New Zealand.

¥	人均消费	RMB200
¥	葡萄酒价格	$ $
	酒单酒款数	78
	杯卖酒数	8
¥	杯卖酒价格	RMB55-95
¥	开瓶费	RMB250
	酒单撰写人	Mr. Max Haahr
	电 话	86 21 54040200
	营业时间	10：00 - 23：00
	地 址	上海市徐汇区安福路 195 号 3 楼
@	网 址	www.mrwillis.com.cn

Mr. Edward Kok Seng Lee

Napa Wine Bar & Kitchen 2007 年成立于上海，汇集各式世界顶级珍馐美馔，拥有全中国酒藏最丰富的酒窖之一。餐厅氛围高雅又不失休闲。在多年的成功经营后，Napa 最近乔迁至著名景点——上海外滩，在新晋餐饮胜地——外滩 22 号续写传奇。

NAPA WINE BAR & KITCHEN

中国年度最佳葡萄酒酒单 – 中国大陆
中国东部地区最佳葡萄酒酒单

酒单大奖专家评审团之酒单点评：

你曾想过点杯波尔多一级庄试试吗？Napa 让你美梦成真。在杯卖酒单上你还能看到 Opus One、滴金堡、优质香槟和众多国际酒款。瓶装酒单则让人叹为观止，每个基本产区都有涉及，从入门款到殿堂级，任君挑选。

Ever dreamed of ordering first growth Bordeaux by-the-glass? Napa Wine Bar and Kitchen has all five on offer, plus Opus One, Ch D'Yquem, fine Champagnes and a smart international selection. The main list is simply spectacular, with all bases covered, from the accessible to the iconic.

欧陆式

¥	人均消费：	RMB500
¥	葡萄酒价格：	$ $ $
🍷	酒单酒款数：	694
🍷	杯卖酒数：	42
¥	杯卖酒价格：	RMB55-1680
¥	开 瓶 费：	RMB300
👤	酒单撰写人：	Mr. Edward Kok Seng Lee
📞	电 话：	86 21 63180057
🕐	营业时间：	12：00 - 14：30（周五至周日）
		18：00 - 23：00
🏠	地 址：	上海中山东二路 22 号 2 楼
@	网 址：	www.napawinebarandkitchen.com

Nene 餐厅位于永福路，它的低调和街道的安静相得益彰，实木镶嵌玻璃窗大气沉稳。白天的它犹如地中海的清新亮丽：粉白的砖墙，怀旧的马赛克地砖，蓝白的主色调橱柜，实木的桌椅，充满了蓬勃的生机；夜晚的 Nene 恰似意大利的浪漫婉约：暗淡的灯光，悠扬的音乐，温暖的烛台，还有经常更换的鲜花，讲述着温馨的隽语。Nene 精于意大利面的烹饪和比萨烤制，得益于正宗的原料、专业的烹调以及到位的服务，让宾客不虚此行。

NENE

意式

酒单大奖专家评审团之酒单点评：

这份酒单就能带你游览一遍意大利的葡萄园。既有常人负担得起的酒款也有顶级意大利佳酿，不论是罕见的 Aglianico 还是常见的霞多丽，你都能寻得到。每款酒还标有酒精度和产区信息以便查阅。

Take a virtual journey through the vineyards of Italy, just by reading the wine list. Plenty of affordable options to match the Italian fare, whether you're after something unusual, like aglianico, or something familiar, like chardonnay. Alcohol levels and regional details provided for each wine.

¥	人均消费	RMB230
¥	葡萄酒价格	$ $
	酒单酒款数	80
	杯卖酒款数	8
¥	杯卖酒价格	RMB88-128
¥	开瓶费	RMB300
	酒单撰写人	Mr. Santo Greco
	电　话	86 21 64185055
	营业时间	11：30 - 14：15；11：30 -01：00 (周末)
		17：30 - 01：00(周一至周五)
	地　址	上海市徐汇区永福路 47 号 106 室
@	网　址	www.nenechina.com

作为上海外滩悦榕庄的主餐厅，优质的服务、丰富的用餐选择、时尚休闲的用餐氛围和健康的饮食搭配是海怡西餐厅的主打特色。餐厅提供一系列本地特色风味、烧烤和招牌菜品。午餐时分，餐厅特别推出精致可口的套餐及商务餐以供选择。每到夜幕降临，这里将化身为典雅浪漫的西式餐厅。宾客可以在这里品尝到肥美鲜嫩的牡蛎、口感醇正的香槟、经典伊朗鱼子酱和精选海鲜拼盘。

OCEANS
海怡西餐厅

法式

酒单大奖专家评审团之酒单点评：

"海怡"是主要提供海鲜的餐厅，所以白葡萄酒的部分有很多可供选择的有趣酒款。芬芳的阿尔萨斯、德国和卢瓦河都是不错的选择。当然，香槟也值得一试，Lallier 和 Armand de Brignac 也被罗列其中。

Oceans is largely devoted to serving seafood and so, it is to the white wine listing where we find some of the more interesting wines. Seek out the delicate white aromatic wines from Alsace, Germany and the Loire. Champagne is well represented too, including Lallier and Armand de Brignac.

¥	人均消费：	RMB320
¥	葡萄酒价格：	$ $ $
	酒单酒款数：	210
¥	杯卖酒数：	14
¥	杯卖酒价格：	RMB50-150
	酒单撰写人：	Mr. Ron Cheng
	电　话：	86 21 25091188
	地　址：	上海市虹口区海平路 19 号
		外滩悦榕庄 1 楼
@	网　址：	www.banyantree.com

位于上海金茂君悦大酒店 56 层的意庐是"食在 56"美食概念的一部分，俯瞰黄浦江两岸陆家嘴及外滩美景，主理意大利菜肴。在开放式厨房，宾客可以观赏厨师精心的烹调艺术，乡村式锈铁架上置满了意大利食品与调料。在开放式厨房的柜台上陈列着各式开胃酒，坐在原始的砂石圆柱旁，尽情享受纯正无比的意大利风味。意庐的所有菜肴都选用最新鲜的原料，加之厨师的娴熟技艺，呈现各具特色的意大利美味。

ON56 - CUCINA ITALIAN RESTAURANT
意庐

酒单大奖专家评审团之酒单点评：

葡萄酒神探总能从酒单上找到深藏的美酒，这是一本值得深度挖掘的酒单。作为一份好的酒单，正如我们预想的一样，这里列出的年份和价格都是值得特别关注的。这份酒单涉及全球，着重意大利酒和法国酒，网罗一些有趣（且有名）的窖藏酒款。找到心头好绝不是难事。

Wine sleuths will find some gems hidden in this list so its worth digging around. As always, be mindful of vintage – and price. A fair international spread with a focus on France and Italy including some interesting (and prestigious) cellar selections. A small prune wouldn't go astray.

意式

¥	人均消费	RMB400-500
¥	葡萄酒价格	$ $ $
	酒单酒款数	235
	杯卖酒款数	18
¥	杯卖酒价格	RMB75-140
	酒单撰写人	Mr. Eric Li
	电　话	86 21 50491234 - 8909
	营业时间	11：30 - 14：30，17：30 - 22：30
	地　址	上海市浦东新区世纪大道 88 号金茂大厦
@	网　址	www.shanghai.grand.hyatt.com

Scarpetta 是一个和食物紧密相连的意大利单词。它的意思是用手拿着面包在盘中漩涡方向把剩余汤汁吸干净。通常，这是在家里面时常出现的画面，而这也恰恰符合 Scarpetta 乡村餐厅风格的定位。

SCARPETTA TRATTORIA

意式

酒单大奖专家评审团之酒单点评：

这是一份精短却夺人眼球的酒单，因为这里展现了意大利当地品种酒的多样性（可口的餐点）。点瓶装酒更好，因为杯卖酒太少。如果这家小餐厅时不时召唤你，请不要惊讶，你每次都能去尝试一个不同的葡萄品种。

Small, but notable - due to its impressive range of Italian varietals (and its delicious menu). Ordering by the bottle is best, as the by-the-glass list is tiny. Don't be surprised if this friendly trattoria beckons you on a regular basis – you can try a different grape variety each time.

¥	人均消费：	RMB300-350
¥	葡萄酒价格：	$ $
🍷	酒单酒款数：	72
🍷	杯卖酒数：	4
¥	杯卖酒价格：	RMB68-98
¥	开瓶费：	RMB248
👤	酒单撰写人：	Mr. Christoffer Backman
☎	电　话：	86 21 33768223
⏰	营业时间：	17：30 - 22：00
🏠	地　址：	上海市黄浦区蒙自路 33 号
@	网　址：	www.scarpetta.cn

坐落于上海最新潮流餐饮地标——思南公馆内的"Shanghai Slim's"是一家大型美式牛排、海鲜西餐厅。餐厅提供特级精选的 14 天干制肉眼牛排，并附有多种牛排可供选择，另有高级小牛肉、羊肉和猪肉。牛肉都是经美国农业部鉴定的高级产品，这在上海堪称顶级。不仅有上好的肉类，餐厅还提供特级精选的龙虾。宾客在一楼海鲜吧台就能亲眼见到养有鲜活的波士顿龙虾的缸。作为本餐厅的第二大招牌产品，龙虾可谓具有举足轻重的地位。经典前餐——龙虾芝士通心粉更是不容错过哟！

SHANGHAI SLIM'S

美式

酒单大奖专家评审团之酒单点评：

众多饱满浓烈型的红葡萄酒可以搭配盘中不同部位的干式熟成牛排。如果你更偏爱波士顿龙虾，那么还有可口的白葡萄酒任君挑选。令人应接不暇地网罗全球酒款的酒单，按照葡萄品种排序，且专注于美国酒。另有 14 款可以杯卖的酒。价格也非常合理。

Plenty of hearty reds to match your 'cut to order' dry-aged steak! Though if Boston lobster is more your style, there are some delicious whites too. A busy, vibrant, global list, arranged by variety, with a particular focus on American wines. 14 by the glass. Prices are very reasonable.

¥	人均消费：	RMB400
¥	葡萄酒价格：	$ $
🍷	酒单酒款数：	100
🍷	杯卖酒款数：	14
¥	杯卖酒价格：	RMB48-88
¥	开瓶费：	RMB180
👤	酒单撰写人：	Mr. David Begg
☎	电　　话：	86 21 64260162
🕐	营业时间：	11：00 - 23：00
🏠	地　　址：	上海市复兴中路 523 弄
		10-12 号 26d

艾利爵士餐厅由之前效力于星级食府——The Dining Room 的法国名厨 David Chauveau 坐镇, 他为艾利爵士餐厅, 酒吧和露台带来出自其手笔的新派法式欧陆菜。餐厅内部装潢以中式红漆陈设, 光亮的木料、乌木墙面及丝绒沙发, 古董及当代陶瓷摆设天衣无缝, 与半岛兼容古今的传统呼应。到达 13 楼后, 宾客即刻融入缤纷的色彩之中, 以此为背景的环形艾利爵士酒吧是餐前浅酌的完美选择。

SIR ELLY'S
艾利爵士餐厅

2014 中国酒单大奖 － 决赛入围名单

现代欧式

酒单大奖专家评审团之酒单点评:

啜一口杯中佳酿, 欣赏秀丽的风景, 研读一下上海最复杂的酒单之一。严格按照产区罗列, 选择有代表性或者新兴酒庄, 涉及全球。勃艮第、波尔多和香槟都精美绝伦。还有精品甜酒值得一试。

Sip fine wine by-the-glass, admire the jaw-dropping view and peruse one of the most sophisticated lists in all of Shanghai. Meticulously organised by region, choose benchmark or emerging producers, from the world over. Burgundy, Bordeaux and Champagne all exceptional. Top dessert wine selection.

¥	人均消费:	RMB800
¥	葡萄酒价格:	$ $ $
	酒单酒款数:	389
♟	杯卖酒数:	24
¥	杯卖酒价格:	RMB110-270
¥	开 瓶 费:	RMB300
	酒单撰写人:	Mr. Jean Claude Terdjemane
☎	电 话:	86 21 23272888
⏰	营业时间:	12:00 - 14:30, 18:00 - 22:30
⌂	地 址:	上海市中山东一路 32 号
		上海半岛酒店 13 层
@	网 址:	www.peninsula.com

Mr. Jerry Liao

推开夏宫设计精美的青铜大门，随处可见的孔雀羽毛元素图案、头顶摇曳的精美丝质灯笼、开放式厨房，无不展示夏宫的典雅、大气。休闲区快速、休闲的用餐理念，结合平易近人的价格，中午主打粤式点心，晚上则以炖汤、烧腊、煲仔为主。中餐行政总厨廖自力师傅自 1986 年就开始接触粤菜，至今已有 27 年之久。国内杰出侍酒师廖唯一先生亲自打造的城中顶级葡萄酒酒单，指定茶艺师现场服务，共同打造顶级中餐盛宴。

SUMMER PALACE
夏宫

粤菜

酒单大奖专家评审团之酒单点评：

另一份静安香格里拉的酒窖酒单。法国的统治地位由顶级勃艮第和波尔多所巩固。来自其他产区的酒则多由知名生产商所提供。一杯罗讷河谷或者勃艮第酒也是不错的尝试。

Another winning combination of wines from the cellars of the Jing An Shangri-La. France reigns supreme with an illustrious range of high-end Burgundy and Bordeaux. The rest of the world is represented by a strong cast of respected producers. Also enjoy Rhone and Burgundian treats by-the-glass.

¥	人均消费	RMB250
¥	葡萄酒价格	$ $ $
	酒单酒款数	328
	杯卖酒数	14
¥	杯卖酒价格	RMB90-240
	酒单撰写人	Mr. Jerry Liao
	电　话	86 21 22036580
	营业时间	11：30 - 14：30（周一至周五）
		10：00 - 15：00（周末）；17：30 - 22：00
	地　址	上海市延安中路 1218 号
		上海静安香格里拉酒店 3 楼
@	网　址	www.jinganshangdining.com

Mr. Xavier Zeng

由 Jason Atherton 主管的外滩第一台是一家现代欧式餐厅。身在其中，宾客可以一种独特的视角观赏到曾经上海最繁华码头——十六铺的景象。餐厅室内装饰有优雅的原木和灰砖，光线充裕。四张原木制成的长条公用餐桌为餐厅增添了温馨的社交氛围。如果就餐于主厅和私人包厢，客人可将十六铺——这座曾经最为繁华的造船厂以及周围的美景尽收眼底。

TABLE NO.1 BY JASON ATHERTON
外滩第一台

现代欧式

酒单大奖专家评审团之酒单点评：

在这份短小且低调的酒单里，很多酒款都让人爱不释手。爱好者们会折服于酒款本身的质量。一款物美价廉的波尔多红就足以说明问题。或者试试 Egon Muller 的雷司令、玛格丽特河的霞多丽，甚至是复杂的 Condrieu。

For a small, understated wine list there is a lot to like. Wine lovers will be pleasantly surprised by the inherent quality of the wines. Try one of the hand-selected, accessibly priced red Bordeauxs. Or perhaps an Egon Muller riesling, Margaret River chardonnay or even a complex condrieu.

¥	人均消费	RMB250-300
¥	葡萄酒价格	＄＄
酒	酒单酒款数	100
♟	杯卖酒数	14
¥	杯卖酒价格	RMB75-105
🧍	酒单撰写人	Mr. Xavier Zeng
☎	电　　话	86 21 60802918
🕐	营业时间	12：00 - 14：30，18：00 - 22：30
🏠	地　　址	上海市黄浦区毛家园路 1-3 号
@	网　　址	www.tableno-1.com

47

1515 牛排馆·酒吧漫不经心地诉说着 20 世纪 20 年代的上海。整个餐厅以老上海电影为主题，经典萦绕在每个角落：入口处的面包房不经意地弥漫着地烘焙香气；主厨 Bradley Hull 自信地翻着 45 天干式发酵的澳洲顶级牛肉；老旧的皮质沙发与厚重的木制桌相得益彰，衬托调酒师 Dario Gentile 的禁酒吧韵味；服务生身着纽约风格的怀旧时装，大摇大摆地服务。

THE 1515 WEST CHOPHOUSE AND BAR
1515 牛排馆 · 酒吧

牛排馆

酒单大奖专家评审团之酒单点评：

与这里的装潢一样，这份酒单也配得上这高档的美国烧烤店，招牌菜是澳大利亚牛肉。优质的酒商比比皆是——时髦的香槟，顶级加州酒和澳洲酒都是特色。怎能少的了法国酒——这里有着整整一页的 DRC。

The wines are as slick as the décor at this upmarket American grill, where the signature Australian beef is the specialty. Quality producers are peppered throughout – highlights include swish Champagnes, top Californian and Australian reds and of course France – including a page of Romanee-Conti.

¥ 人均消费：	RMB500
¥ 葡萄酒价格：	$ $ $
酒单酒款数：	320
杯卖酒款数：	18
¥ 杯卖酒价格：	RMB70-120
酒单撰写人：	Mr. Jerry Liao
电 话：	86 21 22036515
营业时间：	11：30 - 14：30, 18：00 - 22：30
地 址：	上海市延安中路 1218 号
	上海静安香格里拉酒店 4 楼
@ 网 址：	www.jinganshangdining.com

Rainbow Icelandic Halibut
in Five Tastes 五味冰岛比目鱼

ROOSEVELT
WINE CELLAR

Years of laborious work has resulted in the
largest wine cellar in Shanghai
with more than 4,500 labels and 30,000 bottles on premise.
This is our creation of genuine passion for wine.

前排右二 Mr. Yuan Cai Zhao

由美国罗斯福总统家族开发运营的罗斯福公馆是集合美食与佳酿的时尚新地标。位于二楼的罗斯福酒窖存有上海最全面的葡萄酒藏，拥有 4500 余种葡萄酒。精心挑选的 2000 多种涵盖了广泛产区及深度年份的葡萄酒组成了这个令人叹为观止的酒单。位于八楼的罗斯福色戒餐厅坐拥叹为观止的上海外滩景色与融合欧洲高档菜料的丰盛菜式，室内装饰典雅，室外露台尽纳熙攘都市繁华和外滩悠久岁月。

THE HOUSE OF ROOSEVELT
罗斯福公馆

欧陆菜式

酒单大奖专家评审团之酒单点评：

你还在满世界周游并寻找美酒佳酿？在无所不有的罗斯福公馆，你不必如此大费周章了。这里不仅罗列了众所周知的所有勃艮第、波尔多和香槟佳酿，还囊括了几乎所有新世界酒款。请不要忘记在点单前，看看旁边的年份和价格哦！

There's no need to travel the world in search of fine wine – as the House of Roosevelt seems to have it all. You'll be swept away by the inventory of Burgundy, Bordeaux and Champagne, but also by the comprehensive list of new world wines. As always, keep one eye on price, the other on vintage.

¥	人均消费：	RMB800
¥	葡萄酒价格：	$ $ $
🍷	酒单酒款数：	1901
🍷	杯卖酒款数：	33
¥	杯卖酒价格：	RMB90-170
¥	开瓶费：	RMB 350
👤	酒单撰写人：	Mr. Zane Zhao
📞	电　　话：	86 21 23220888
🕐	营业时间：	11：30-14：30,18：00-22：30
🏠	地　　址：	上海市黄浦区中山东一路 27 号
@	网　　址：	www.27bund.com

意大利名厨 Salvatore Cuomo 在全球已经拥有 60 多家餐厅，包括日本东京、韩国首尔等都市，The Kitchen 是他在上海开设的真正意义上的第一家外国餐厅。整个餐厅设于黄浦江边休闲公园内的透明玻璃屋内，宾客可以坐在东方明珠底下，尽情观赏美丽的黄浦江景致。如果遇上不错的天气，不妨到原木装点的露台上找个座位，感受周围的迷人美景。到了冬季，宾客便可以望着外面寒风吹扫着江面，自己却窝在温暖舒适的室内一边品饮美酒佳酿，一边享用意大利美食。

THE KITCHEN BY SALVATORE CUOMO

意式

酒单大奖专家评审团之酒单点评：

这份酒单的亮点在于意大利酒，它很好地覆盖了从托斯卡纳到皮埃蒙特的各个意大利产区。其他国家的酒款起着补充作用。这里有很多性价比高的杯卖酒，但是瓶装酒款更加有趣。

The strength of this list lies in the diversity of Italian wines, arranged by region, with a good spread from Tuscany and Piedmont. All other countries play a somewhat supporting role. There's a sound selection of affordable wines by-the-glass though the by-the-bottle offering is more interesting.

- 人均消费：RMB400-500
- 葡萄酒价格：$ $
- 酒单酒款数：250
- 杯卖酒数：10
- 杯卖酒价格：RMB78-138
- 开 瓶 费：RMB300
- 酒单撰写人：Mr. Calvin Chen
- 电　　话：86 21 50541265
- 营业时间：11：00 - 23：00
- 地　　址：上海市浦东新区陆家嘴西路 2967 号 D 座
- 网　　址：www.ystable.com

Mr. Kobe Hou

扒餐厅是一家牛排馆及烧烤餐厅，具有时尚现代的氛围。餐厅为宾客们供应上海首屈一指的顶级食草牛肉，包括在"醒肉房"中展示的特色"澳洲神户战斧牛排"。宾客可尽情享用海鲜烧烤、美味菜肴以及精选出的各种新世界和旧世界葡萄酒。餐厅设有适合举办派对和庆典的私人用餐包房。

THE MEAT
扒餐厅

牛排馆

酒单大奖专家评审团之酒单点评：

从高质量的杯卖单，你就能看出整个酒单的基调——平衡且广泛。众多经典的法国酒、意大利酒以及知名的新世界酒足以匹配这份肉食者菜单。标志性的勃艮第和波尔多在这里诱惑着葡萄酒爱好者们。

The quality by-the-glass selection sets the tone for what is a balanced and extensive wine list. Plenty of classic French and Italians, to complement the carnivorous menu, plus a respectable new world offering. Iconic Burgundies and Bordeauxs are there to tempt or tease.

¥	人均消费：	RMB550
¥	葡萄酒价格：	$ $ $
▮	酒单酒款数：	190
♀	杯卖酒数：	26
¥	杯卖酒价格：	RMB88-198
¥	开瓶费	禁止外带酒水
☺	酒单撰写人：	Mr. Kobe Hou
☏	电　　话：	86 21 61698888-6322
⏱	营业时间：	17：30 - 22：00
⌂	地　　址：	上海市浦东花木路1388号
		浦东嘉里大酒店2楼
@	网　　址：	www.thecookthemeatthebrew.com

普朗姆生蚝吧是中国第一家真正意义上的生蚝酒吧。酒吧从世界各地进口数十种新鲜的生蚝生食，并为宾客选搭非常独特的葡萄酒、令人惊讶的杜松子酒以及各类金酒、啤酒、鸡尾酒等。当然，除了生蚝美食外，这里也是一个独一无二的休闲小憩之所。顶层露台和大阳台的绝妙景色，在美妙的爵士乐背景的烘托下，配合柔美的灯光与温馨的陈设一定能让宾客意犹未尽。能容纳 16-20 人的户外庭院也是朋友聚会、派对的最佳选择。

THE PLUMP OYSTER
普朗姆生蚝吧

酒单大奖专家评审团之酒单点评：

在这个怡人的生蚝吧，享用新鲜的生蚝、优质的葡萄酒和烈酒吧。这份酒单就是为了菜单而生，包括许多适合生蚝的酒款、一系列气泡酒和清爽的红葡萄酒。纯正、华丽、香气四溢的白葡萄酒尽在酒单之上。

Enjoy freshly-shucked oysters, fine wine and spirits at this atmospheric oyster lounge. The wine list has been appropriately tailored to the menu, including a dedicated page on oyster-friendly wines, plus a spread of bubblies and light reds. A good selection of pure, bright, expressive whites.

意式和海鲜

¥	人均消费	RMB300-500
¥	葡萄酒价格：	$ $
♗	酒单酒款数：	86
♟	杯卖酒数：	7
¥	杯卖酒价格：	RMB69-179
¥	开瓶费：	RMB180
♟	酒单撰写人：	Mr. Chao Wan
☎	电　话	86 21 54183175
◷	营业时间：	18：00 - 02：00
⌂	地　　址：	上海市建国中路 169 号 3 楼
@	网　　址：	www.theplumpoyster.com

在 Unico by Mauro Colagreco, 阿根廷籍米其林二星厨师 Mauro Colagreco 使用自己的有机农场的新鲜季节性有机蔬菜，在尊重食材的基础上烹饪出简单创意的精致美食，带给食客一场全新的烹饪旅程。所有的佳肴都采用上等季节性的食材烹饪，保证了其原汁原味，反映其慷慨分享的理念。多次获奖的鸡尾酒奇才 Hektor Monroy，在 Unico by Mauro Colagreco 的鸡尾酒创作中注入了拉丁的激情、灵魂和创造力。又以烹饪团队为灵感，Hektor Monroy 创作出包含多样性口味的创意拉丁鸡尾酒。

UNICO BY MAURO COLAGRECO
优尼客

拉丁式

酒单大奖专家评审团之酒单点评：

与众不同的酒单如同炎炎夏日的一抹清泉。以阿根廷酒为主打的酒单更是令人兴奋——每个产区都附上了相应的建议，还有一系列可供选择的马尔贝克。剩下的部分也值得表扬，不论是生产商还是产区，你总能寻到亮点。

It's refreshing to see a list beating to the sound of its own drum. The focus on wines from Argentina is relevant and exciting – there are some regional suggestions upfront plus a good range of malbecs. The rest of the list is commendable, with producer and regional spotlights dotted throughout.

¥	人均消费	RMB350-1000
¥	葡萄酒价格：	$ $ $
	酒单酒款数：	260
♆	杯卖酒数：	14
¥	杯卖酒价格：	RMB88-238
¥	开 瓶 费：	RMB300
♘	酒单撰写人：	Mr. Junbin Qin
☎	电 话：	86 21 53085399
⏰	营业时间：	18：00 - 02：00
⌂	地 址：	上海市黄浦区中山东一路
		外滩三号 2 楼
@	网 址：	www.unico.cn.com

非常时髦餐厅是一个经典欧洲式餐厅，以私人居家式概念为灵感而设计。餐厅内设为宽敞明亮的"厨房"、多姿多彩的"书房"与温馨舒适的"客厅"，处处营造居家的惬意氛围。餐厅提供地道的欧陆式美味佳肴，注重纯正配方并运用新鲜原料。餐厅的标志性特色是厨师们在餐桌边现场烹饪出宾客所点佳肴，而宾客在与餐厅厨师现场烹饪的互动中可以零距离地体验到烹饪的艺术。

VUE RESTAURANT
非常时髦餐厅

酒单大奖专家评审团之酒单点评：

被列入其中的知名酒款让人倍感欣慰，这份酒单的优势在于红葡萄酒部分，来自澳大利亚、意大利和西班牙的红葡萄酒或是新西兰的吉布利特砾石区西拉都是不错的选择。选择顶级波尔多的需要仔细考虑年份是否合适。

Take comfort in the presence of the recognisable labels, with the list being stronger in reds than whites. Some dependable Australian, Italian and Spanish reds – or try a Gimblett Gravels Syrah from NZ. Prestigious Bordeaux for those who choose – though consider vintage carefully across the board.

欧式

¥	人均消费：	RMB700
¥	葡萄酒价格：	$ $ $
🍷	酒单酒款数：	190
🍷	杯卖酒数：	19
¥	杯卖酒价格：	RMB95-250
👤	酒单撰写人：	Mr. Edouard Demptos
☎	电　话：	86 21 63931234-6328
⏰	营业时间：	11：30-14：30（周一至周五）；
		11：30-15：00（周日早午餐）；18：00-23：00
🏠	地　址：	上海市虹口区黄浦路 199 号外滩茂
		悦酒店西楼 30 层
@	网　址：	www.shanghai.bund.hyatt.com

湖滨 28 中餐厅由具有丰富经验的名厨汲取名菜之精华，提供原汁原味的杭州菜、淮扬菜、苏州菜等江南主要菜系，不仅口味纯正，而且讲求营养和健康。原料和配料均具有鲜活的品质，每一个细节都有专人把关，以确保菜肴的品质。菜单上的菜式更是经过反复尝试和提炼而成，注重刀工和火候，抛开过量的装饰和调味，返璞归真，这些都真正体现了经典江南菜式历久弥新的魅力。

28 HUBIN ROAD
湖滨 28 中餐厅

杭帮菜式

酒单大奖专家评审团之酒单点评：

复杂详尽的酒单与美丽精致的杭帮菜是这个高级餐厅最好的〝软实力〞。对澳大利亚和新西兰酒款精准的挑选完全不逊于以法国为主的旧世界酒款。杯卖酒单也同样令人满意。

A sophisticated list to match the refined and beautiful Hangzhou dishes served at this highly respected restaurant. The astute selection of Australian and New Zealand wines sit comfortably alongside old world classics, mainly French. The by-the-glass is satisfying.

¥	人均消费：	RMB300
¥	葡萄酒价格：	$ $ $
酒	酒单酒款数：	163
♉	杯卖酒款数：	26
¥	杯卖酒价格：	RMB60
♙	酒单撰写人：	Mr. Jan Stoverink
☎	电　　话：	86 571 87791234
⏰	营业时间：	11：30-14：30, 17：30-22：00
⌂	地　　址：	杭州市湖滨路 28 号
@	网　　址：	www.hangzhou.regency.hangzhou.cn

西湖餐厅位于酒店一层，全天候供应早、午、晚餐，为客人呈献亚洲各国风味美食。餐厅设计别具匠心，传统的石墙、精致的地板与晶莹的餐具彼此交融。特设户外用餐区，荷塘翠竹，景致怡人，是良朋聚首、开怀畅饮的好去处。

WL BISTRO
西湖餐厅

亚洲菜式

酒单大奖专家评审团之酒单点评：

不论是见多识广的葡萄酒爱好者还是想为佳肴点一杯佐餐的食客，这份酒单一定不会让你失望。精选的波尔多和顶级托斯卡纳都是它的亮点，同为亮点的还有来自山西和宁夏的葡萄酒。

For discerning wine enthusiasts, or those seeking a fantastic complement to the fine dining on offer, there's lots to enjoy in this list. Highlights include keenly-chosen Bordeaux and premium Tuscan wines, joined by an intriguing and neat selection of local wines from Shanxi and Ningxia provinces.

¥	人均消费：	RMB250
¥	葡萄酒价格：	$ $
	酒单酒款数：	182
	杯卖酒款数：	10
¥	杯卖酒价格：	RMB110-210
¥	开瓶费：	RMB500
	酒单撰写人：	Mr. Johnson Hu
	电　话：	86 571 88298888
	营业时间：	12：00 - 22：00
	地　址：	杭州市灵隐路 5 号
@	网　址：	www.fourseasons.com/hangzhou

坐拥东钱湖美景的悦轩餐厅是一间具有居家风格的全日餐厅。客人可在开放式的厨房选取自助早餐，午餐及晚餐汇集了各种精选单点餐和特色美酒，雅致的中式佳肴和地道的西式美食供宾客选择。"藏酒馆"拥有数量惊人的葡萄酒，配备了大型烤箱的开放式厨房更可让宾客现场欣赏到厨师的烹饪过程。客人在舒适优雅的环境中，尽情享受原汁原味的中西特色美食。

DINING ROOM
悦轩

西式、中式

酒单大奖专家评审团之酒单点评：

酒单不长，但每款都是精选佳酿。它不仅囊括新旧世界生产商，还有一些产区的代表之作，比如加州金粉黛或马尔堡黑皮诺。撰写人对葡萄酒了若指掌。众多令人惊艳的开胃酒和餐后酒。

It's not a huge list, but there's thoughtful selection that sees not only new and old world producers listed, but some of their best regional assets, like zinfandel of California or Marlborough pinot noir. Confidently curated. Aperitif and digestif listings are an impressive and lengthy highlight.

¥	人均消费：	RMB300
¥	葡萄酒价格：	$ $
♠	酒单酒款数：	24
♟	杯卖酒数：	5
¥	杯卖酒价格：	RMB90-150
☎	电　话：	86 574 28881234
◷	营业时间：	11：30 - 22：00
⌂	地　址：	宁波市东钱湖大堰路 188 号
		宁波柏悦酒店
@	网　址：	www.ningbo.park.hyatt.com

Mr. Tank Tan

龙虾酒吧扒房已历经几十年发展以至臻完美的食谱为宾客奉上各种国际饕餮美食。新鲜的海鲜、烤肉以及面点，搭配由专业侍酒师精选的顶级佐餐酒，为用餐客人带来难忘的用餐体验。龙虾酒吧扒房设有一个长廊酒吧，采用大理石、桃花心木和皮革等材料，装修风格时尚典雅。餐厅设有室内、室外及私人用餐区以便宾客选择，并安排爵士、拉丁流行乐等晚间现场音乐表演。

LOBSTER BAR AND GRILL
龙虾酒吧扒房

欧式

酒单大奖专家评审团之酒单点评：

DRC 的酒款让人印象深刻，但是覆盖诸多优质产区、有深度的酒款更值得回味。法国酒是重中之重，但是澳大利亚酒、美国酒、意大利酒和西班牙酒也独具特色。你在这儿一定能喝到好酒！

Listings of super producer Domaine de la Romanée-Conti are very impressive, but so is the overall depth of the list that sources wines from all over great wine producing regions. French wines are most important here, but luxury wines from Australia, USA, Italy and Spain also feature. Good drinking.

¥	人均消费：	RMB400
♥	葡萄酒价格：	$ $
♠	酒单酒款数：	145
♟	杯卖酒款数：	25
¥	杯卖酒价格：	RMB45-235
☺	酒单撰写人：	Mr. Tank Tan
☎	电　话：	86 574 87998888
⏰	营业时间：	17：30 - 22：00
🏠	地　址：	宁波市江东区豫源街 88 号
@	网　址：	www.shangri-la.com

盛宴西餐厅是以法式西餐为特色的餐厅。来自法国的行政总厨及其带领的厨师团队精心地为每一位客人烹制可口的菜肴。餐厅每天晚上都会为客人准备海鲜盛宴，特别是周五到周日的晚餐，让每一位来到餐厅的客人尽情享受食物的美味与服务的周到。

FEAST
盛宴

法式

酒单大奖专家评审团之酒单点评：

虽然酒单聚合了一些世界优质产区和有内涵的生产商，但是这些中国葡萄酒、白酒和米酒所占比重之大又为其增添了一份神秘感。非常值得发掘的酒单。

While the list showcases some of the world's great wine regions, and a depth of premier producers, it's the lengthy listing of local Chinese wines supported by excellent Chinese rice wine and 'Bai Jui' Liqueurs, that adds an extra 'x-factor'. A great exploration.

 人均消费： RMB400-500

 葡萄酒价格： $ $

酒单酒款数： 154

杯卖酒款数： 32

杯卖酒价格： RMB78-138

开 瓶 费： RMB300

酒单撰写人： Mr. Fankie Lui

电　　话： 86 572 2299999

营业时间： 06：30 - 23：00

地　　址： 湖州市太湖路 5858 号
喜来登温泉度假酒店

网　　址： www.sheraton.com

MR. METICULOUS KNOWS THAT
THE CONTENTS OF YOUR GLASS CAN BE
A GREAT CHARACTER REFERENCE.

Petaluma Fine Wines - Meticulously made in Australia
"葡萄之路"精品葡萄酒,来自澳大利亚的完美佳酿!

2013
KNAPPSTEIN
HAND PICKED RIESLING

- · 100% Riesling from the Clare Valley
- · Sourced from vineyards in the Watervale sub-region of the Clare Valley, including our Ackland vineyard. Vine ages range from approx. 10-30 years old

94 Points
"Youthful musky perfume, lemon, bath salts, vanilla. Intense flavour, lemon drops, core of tingly acidity, light chalky and flinty character on the finish."
Gary Walsh, Winefront

93 Points
"Crisp and tense, a knife edge of lemony acidity but packed with juicy green apple fruit and that subtle kiss of floral perfume. So enjoyable."
Mike Bennie, WBM

93 Points
"2013 is a tightly honed vintage for Knappstein, precise in its lemon zest and lime juice definition and granny smith apple crunch. Alluring notes of fennel and anise fill out a concentrated and persistent palate. An impressive riesling."
Tyson Stelzer, WINE TASTE

"Pure, deep peel and icy water as pristine as young riesling gets. And the same in the mouth too with building fruit and deep. Month-watering acidity etched into the gentle chewiness."
Tim White, AFR

"A sheer delight, from one of the Clare's most distinguished producers. It features aromatic lemon and lime, on the nose and palate, and zippy acidity – crisp, dry and bouncing with vitality."
Kerry Skinner, Illawarra Mercury

廿九阁为宾客提供京城稀缺的世界级优质奶酪和冷切肉类等精选美味，意大利帕尔马风干火腿、西班牙伊比利亚风干猪后腿、意大利风干萨拉米肠、蜂蜜猪腩肉等众多西式扒类，还有在酒窖中甄选出来的陈年佳酿，为喜爱肉类与品酒的男士或是真我个性的女士打造独具一格的就餐体验。

29 GRILL RESTAURANT
廿九阁

西式

酒单大奖专家评审团之酒单点评：

杯卖酒款覆盖全球，还包括一些优秀且少见的生产商。而酒单本身则涵盖了世上每个生产优质葡萄酒的产区。Alto Adige、波尔多和华丽的香槟都是不容忽视的亮点。

An excellent by-the-glass list traverses the globe and some very fine, less-seen producers, while the body of the list manages to delight with all-corners-of-globe exploration of fine wine producing regions. Alto Adige to a neatly chosen selection of Bordeaux and some fancy Champagne are highlights.

¥	人均消费：	RMB340
¥	葡萄酒价格：	$ $
	酒单酒款数：	180
	杯卖酒数：	17
	酒单撰写人：	Mr. Remi Torres
	电　话：	86 10 65846300
	营业时间：	11：30 - 14：30（周一至周五）
		18：00 - 22：00（周一至周六）
	地　址：	北京市朝阳区东三环北路29号
		康莱德酒店2楼
@	网　址：	www.beijing.conradhotels.com

热情又精致时髦——这里有获奖大厨 Jordi Valles 烹制的充满活力的现代派风格美食、时尚优雅的室内装饰，灵感来自西班牙天然木材的纹理质感及其褐色的温暖舒适。在三里屯的那里花园——西班牙文化爱好者的朝拜中心，Agua 与周围环境浑然一体，散发着独特迷人的西班牙魅力。Agua 餐厅专注于独具地中海特色的现代西班牙菜，崇尚自然口味。芬芳的香草、至浓至醇的初榨橄榄油与最新鲜优质的食材的完美结合，呈现出原汁原味的西班牙精髓。

AGUA

西班牙式

酒单大奖专家评审团之酒单点评：

西班牙菜系的餐厅怎能少了西班牙酒，这张酒单对西班牙酒的覆盖面足够广，涉及多种风格。一些其他国家的酒也穿插其中。酒单上的餐酒足以搭配其饮食，佳酿也不缺。

The food menu is of course Spanish so there's no disappointment in seeing the breadth of Spain heavily represented in this list. There's lots of diversity in Spanish styles and a smattering of international interlopers for good measure. Great choices for cuisine, with fine wines also in the mix.

¥	人均消费	RMB400
¥	葡萄酒价格：	$
	酒单酒款数：	94
	杯卖酒款数：	12
¥	杯卖酒价格：	RMB70-95
¥	开 瓶 费：	RMB250
	酒单撰写人：	Mr. Marc Font
	电　　话：	86 10 52086188
	营业时间：	12：00 - 14：30, 18：00 - 22：30
	地　　址：	北京市朝阳区三里屯北街81号那里花园4楼
@	网　　址：	www.aqua.com.hk

阿丽雅是中国大饭店频获嘉奖的旗舰餐厅，具有现代欧式烹饪风格，拥有极其丰富的世界各年份葡萄酒，在北京业内被认定为最佳餐厅。悠闲轻松的氛围非常适合品酒用餐，新鲜肥嫩的牛肉及海鲜产品也不容错过。主餐厅位于3层，配备有3间贵宾间，开放式厨房方便宾客观赏到现场烹饪精彩演示。

ARIA RESTAURANT
阿丽雅

现代欧式

酒单大奖专家评审团之酒单点评：

只要有 JJP 雷司令在，那么这样的酒单一定很受欢迎，更不用说那些位于金字塔顶端的众多生产商和酒款了。1976 年香槟王"珍藏"打头阵，波尔多和勃艮第紧随其后。优质酒款的可选范围很宽泛。

Anywhere that pours JJ Prum riesling by-the-glass will instantly win friends, then the list cascades into a who's who of top-end wine producers and marquee wines. Dom Perignon "Oenotheque" 1976 a start, but great listings of Bordeaux and Burgundy follow. Broad selection of excellent wines here.

¥	人均消费	RMB300
¥	葡萄酒价格	$ $ $
👫	酒单酒款数	514
🍷	杯卖酒数	28
¥	杯卖酒价格	RMB95-230
👤	酒单撰写人	Mr. Gary Zhang
📞	电　话	86 10 65052266-5743
🕐	营业时间	11：30 - 14：30（周一至周五）
		17：30 - 22：00（周一至周日）
🏠	地　址	北京市朝阳区建国门外大街一号中国大饭店大堂层
@	网　址	www.shangri-la.com

以意大利皇冠酒区"巴罗洛"命名的餐厅，处处洋溢着意大利的浪漫与热情。融合传统与现代菜品的精髓，带来焕然一新的体验。美食与美酒的完美搭配，打造致臻享受。开放式厨房设计，尽享与厨师间的完美互动。特别设置的私密就餐空间，营造出尊享的专属感。

Mr. Larry Yang

BAROLO
巴罗洛

意式

酒单大奖专家评审团之酒单点评：

20 世纪 50 年代的波尔多酒绝对能让你合不拢嘴，华丽的侍酒师之选涵盖了全球顶级酒款。这是一份质量与和谐并重的酒单，能与菜单阴阳调和，值得细细琢磨。

A jaw-dropping selection of vintage Bordeaux stretching back to the 1950s is a highlight, but the epic Sommeliers Collection is equal to task with great wines of the world. This is a lengthy list of quality and global awareness, fine-tuned to the delightful food menu. A list to pore over.

💰	人均消费：	RMB500
🍷	葡萄酒价格：	$ $ $
🍴	酒单酒款数：	500
🍷	杯卖酒数：	10
💰	杯卖酒价格：	RMB80-398
💰	开瓶费：	RMB300
👤	酒单撰写人：	Mr. Larry Yang
📞	电　　话：	86 10 59088151
🕐	营业时间：	11：30 - 14：00，18：00 - 22：00
🏠	地　　址：	北京市朝阳区华贸中心建国路甲 83 号
		北京丽思·卡尔顿酒店二层
@	网　　址：	www.ritzcarlton.com/zh-cn/properties/
		beijing/dining/barolo/default.htm

"荣尊 1893"设计典雅奢华，为顾客提供精致的国际美食。荣尊 1893 以纽约第一家华尔道夫酒店的开业年份命名，传承了 1893 年纽约华尔道夫的繁华，完美地继承了其独到的烹饪精髓。当厨师们在烹制精美的特色美食时，宾客能够在开放式厨房中与他们亲密交流，漫游美食国度。荣尊 1893 可容纳 70 名宾客，包括可供 8 人用餐的展示包间。餐厅中最引人注目的莫过于店中央的开放式厨房。宾客可散坐四处，啜饮美酒，通过食与视充分参与美食体验。

BRASSERIE 1893
荣尊 1893

西式

酒单大奖专家评审团之酒单点评：

这是一份更注重质量而不是价格的酒单，因此你总能找得到世界顶级酒庄。引人注目的是西班牙酒的深度和罕见的卢瓦河与勃艮第酒款，霞多丽是酒单上当之无愧的霸主。这份酒单品位不俗。

It seems the list focuses on quality rather than affordable wines, and therefore showcases some of the great producers of the world. Of particular interest is the depth of Spanish wine and rare wines of Loire and Burgundy, with chardonnay a hero on this menu. There's plenty to relish here.

人均消费：	RMB300-400
葡萄酒价格：	$ $
酒单酒款数：	359
杯卖酒款数：	21
杯卖酒价格：	RMB85-195
酒单撰写人：	Mr. Pieter Ham
电　话：	86 10 85208989
营业时间：	11：30-14：30, 17：30-22：00
地　址：	北京市东城区金鱼胡同 5-15 号
网　址：	beijing.waldorfastoria.com

被 "*The Daily Meal*" 杂志评选为 "2013 年度亚洲最佳餐厅第五名" 的前门 M 餐厅坐拥逾 600 年历史的前门大街——京城最著名、最繁华的商业中心。无论在露台还是餐厅里享用佳肴，你都能欣赏到前门和紫禁城，甚至是天安门广场的绝美景致。餐厅为饕客们营造了坐享美食与美景的优雅氛围，感受北京的历史积淀与摩登时尚。前门 M 餐厅供应高品质的现代欧陆菜肴，与上海最受欢迎的米氏西餐厅以及坐拥迷人夜景的魅力酒吧，共同抒写了米氏餐饮的京沪传奇。

CAPITAL M
前门 M 餐厅

现代欧式

酒单大奖专家评审团之酒单点评：

这份酒单分为精简版和完整版，它的创新性还体现在对所谓"新世界"生产商的偏好。优质香槟和一些精品澳洲酒无疑是它的亮点。除了杯卖以外，这里的葡萄酒还可以按卡拉夫瓶（375ml）卖。

Divided into 'short list' and 'long list', this innovative wine menu has a decided leaning to what could be considered 'New World' producers. Highlights however are great Champagne and some excellent Australian boutique producers. As a bonus wines are available by selected glass and carafe too.

¥	人均消费：	RMB368
¥	葡萄酒价格：	$ $
酒单酒款数：	300
♟	杯卖酒数：	20
¥	杯卖酒价格：	RMB60-140
♟	酒单撰写人：	Mr. Zi Zheng Xu
☎	电　　话：	86 10 67022727
⏰	营业时间：	11：30 - 14：30（周一至周五）；
		11：30 - 17：00（周末）；18：00 - 22：30
⌂	地　　址：	北京市前门步行街 2 号 3 层
@	网　　址：	www.m-restaurant-group.com

位于北京金融街丽思卡尔顿酒店一层的意味轩屡获大奖，曾被福布斯（Forbes）等多家有影响力的媒体评为最优秀意大利餐厅。餐厅精选地道的意大利北部佳肴以及海鲜、禽肉类等意大利北部特色美味。餐厅赋予现代设计亦不失华贵。以深红色的樱桃木为架构，特制镀银餐具及各种瓷器用品均出自意大利名家之手。正面墙布采用拉丁仿古设计，红色的孟买风格窗帘以及名贵的水晶灯造就与众不同的就餐氛围。

CÉPE RESTAURANT
意味轩餐厅

酒单大奖专家评审团之酒单点评：

尽管如此之多的意大利酒出现在一份酒单上很是令人惊讶，但令人愉悦的是它能与餐厅的菜系相搭配。爱好者们在看到 Angelo Gaja 的数个酒款后一定欣喜不已，尽管酒单上的明星酒款不在少数。法国酒的选择同样值得赞扬。

Impressive focus on Italian wines found in this list, and wholly appropriate considering the cuisines of the restaurant. Wine lovers will no doubt enjoy the lengthy cellar list of Angelo Gaja's magnificent wines, though there's plenty of stars throughout the list. Wines of France are also impressive.

意式

¥	人均消费：	RMB1000
¥	葡萄酒价格：	$ $
♟	酒单酒款数：	356
♟	杯卖酒数：	22
¥	杯卖酒价格：	RMB88-398
¥	开瓶费：	RMB300
♟	酒撰写人：	Mr. Daniel Deng
☎	电　话：	86 10 66296996
⏰	营业时间：	11：30 - 14：30，17：30 - 22：30
⌂	地　址：	北京市西城区金城坊东街1号
		金融街丽思卡尔顿酒店一层
@	网　址：	www.ritzcarlton.com/hotels/beijing_financial

意式传统餐厅迪卡博提供热情亲切的意式服务与精致味美的现代西式美膳。迪卡博的午餐氛围自在活泼，到了傍晚日落时，清闲惬意的轻松气息浓厚。不管何时用餐，宾客都能享有主厨所准备的最新鲜食材、最色香诱人的顶级美食以及率性且殷勤的用餐服务。意大利式的热情将给予宾客一个难以忘怀的餐饮体验。

DACCAPO
迪卡博

酒单大奖专家评审团之酒单点评：

这是一张满是顶级酒款的酒单，神恩山、Solaia 和 Bollinger RD（1997 年和 1999 年）让它无比华丽。虽然简单易饮的酒款较少，但是仅有的那些酒款都是高性价比之作，值得一试。

The list is set decidedly to the premium; lengthy in big name wines like Henschke's Hill Of Grace, Solaia and Bollinger RD (1997 and 1999!) making this an impressive and fancy wine offering. There's less in the easy-drinking section but what's been selected is undoubtedly worthy too.

意式

¥	人均消费：	RMB400-500
¥	葡萄酒价格：	$ $
	酒单酒款数：	89
	杯卖酒数：	25
¥	杯卖酒价格：	RMB60-1000
¥	开 瓶 费：	RMB200
	酒单撰写人：	Mr. Richard Pirsch
	电　　话：	86 10 85221888
	营业时间：	11：30 - 14：30, 18：00 - 22：00
	地　　址：	北京市东城区金宝街 99 号丽晶酒店
@	网　　址：	www.regenthotels.com/en/beijing

国贸 79 是北京顶尖的国际酒店餐厅之一。因为宾客可在此纵览故宫壮丽景象，所以这里是一个可以享用国际美食的迷人目的地。就餐者可在这家时尚的餐厅里品尝用简单的新鲜食材烹制而成的美味佳肴。

GRILL 79
国贸 79

现代欧式

酒单大奖专家评审团之酒单点评：

这份有代表性的酒单从一而终，不仅选取了世界级的酒款、新兴的产区和葡萄酒风格，还包含顶级生产商之作。从小农香槟到勃艮第佳酿，再到卢瓦河谷、澳大利亚和罗讷河谷的车库酒，这是一份非常特别的酒单。

Exemplary list curated with a clear vision to represent a global wine program, emerging wine regions and styles, and champion prestige wines and producers. From grower/producer Champagne to fine Burgundy and back to cult wine producers of Loire, Australia or Rhone, a very special and long list.

¥	人均消费：	RMB900
¥	葡萄酒价格：	$ $ $
🍷	酒单酒款数：	620
🍷	杯卖酒数：	23
¥	杯卖酒价格：	RMB75-180
👤	酒单撰写人：	Mr. Max Hohenwarter
☎	电　话：	86 10 65052299
⏱	营业时间：	12：00 - 14：00，18：00 - 22：00
🏠	地　址：	北京建国门外大街 1 号
@	网　址：	www.shangri-la.com/beijing/ chinaworldsummitwing/dining/restaurants

来福士酒店的旗舰餐厅——家安是北京最佳法式餐厅之一，提供清淡、创新的法式餐饮，紧跟时代的步伐。优质的法国酒和新世界葡萄酒为您带来绝妙的用餐体验。

JAAN RESTAURANT
家安

法式

酒单大奖专家评审团之酒单点评：

一份以日常易饮的酒款开始的酒单很难不让人喜欢，紧随而来的是奇珍异宝的"大师精选"，比如澳大利亚老藤、正当季的波尔多。用一杯罕见的 Vin de Constance 来收尾吧。这是一份选择精准的酒单。

There's lots to like about a wine list that shows convenient, everyday kind of drinking list then steps it up to a 'Master List' filled with vinous gems, like a selection of fine Australian old-vine wines and plenty from smart Bordeaux producers, finishing with the rare Vin De Constance. Sharp list

¥	人均消费：	RMB480
¥	葡萄酒价格：	$ $
酒单酒款数：		200
杯卖酒数：		12
酒单撰写人：		Mr. Shuang Chen
电　话：		86 10 85004331
营业时间：		18：30 - 22：30（周日休）
地　址：		北京市东长安街 33 号
网　址：		www.raffles.com/beijing

　　"Mio" 在意大利文解作"我的"。Mio 内设开放式厨房及传统比萨烤炉，名副其实地让您体会到宾至如归的感受。餐厅主打意大利南部菜式，包括比萨、意大利面及传统餐前小吃。Mio 采用新鲜时令食材炮制佳肴美食，根据季节转变不时推出新款菜式。餐厅亮点为优质上乘的地中海美食，前菜包括酥脆小螯虾配西班牙凉菜和鳄梨，精选主菜则有炖小牛颊配胡萝卜泥、甜豆及脆米，阿拉斯加鳕鱼配红椒汁和圣丹尼尔火腿粉。采用正宗烤炉焗制的自家比萨也是餐厅主要菜式之一，包括生帕尔玛火腿比萨、水牛芝士比萨、番茄比萨及芝麻菜比萨。

MIO, FOUR SEASONS HOTEL BEIJING
北京四季酒店 MIO 餐厅

酒单大奖专家评审团之酒单点评：

这份明智的酒单包揽了世界众多知名产区，亮点在于精选酒款：魅力香槟、法国贵族、意大利名酒、名门之后和明日之星。这里都是一些不乏历史悠久且新奇有趣的酒款。这是一份值得深究的酒单。

A brilliant list that travels to the great wine regions of the world, but the highlight are the collections, unusually named Champagne Glamour, Nobles de France, Italian Big Boys, The New Generation and The Future - here the list shines with incredible wines of pedigree and interest. Dig in.

意式

¥	人均消费	RMB600
¥	葡萄酒价格	$ $ $
🍷	酒单酒款数	500
🍷	杯卖酒数	16
¥	杯卖酒价格	RMB70-178
¥	开瓶费	RMB400
👤	酒单撰写人	Mr. Wifried Sentex
☎	电　话	86 10 56958522
🕐	营业时间	11：30 - 14：00，17：30 - 22：00
🏠	地　　址	北京市朝阳区亮马桥路 48 号 四季酒店三层
@	网　址	www.fourseasons.com/beijing/dining/restaurants/mio

莫尔顿牛排坊一贯秉承创始人的远见，即恪守严格标准，烹饪顶级美食，确保真材实料，提供优质服务，让客人在舒适的环境中享用佳肴。凭借 34 年丰富经验，在美国高级食肆中享负盛名，独占鳌头。坐落于繁华的金宝街地段，同时拥有 8 间私人宴会厅以及专为美酒鉴赏家而设的宽敞私人酒廊。

MORTON'S OF CHICAGO THE STEAK HOUSE BEIJING
莫尔顿牛排坊 － 北京

酒单大奖专家评审团之酒单点评：

欢迎来到莫尔顿牛排坊，这里是鸡尾酒爱好者的天堂。各种伏特加，金酒，其它主题的鸡尾酒也应有尽有。对了，优质的美国酒可以搭配盘中的牛排和薯条。能装 6 盎司的酒杯与德克萨斯的一样大，红酒爱好者绝对能过足瘾。这是一份包罗万象的酒单。

Welcome to Morton's Steak House the home of spa-tinis, vodka and gintinis and general "tini" madness. Oh, and some seriously good American wines to go with your steak and fries. Wine glass sizes are as big as Texas (six ounces) and red drinkers will be in seventh heaven. A strong, all-rounder list.

美式

¥	人均消费：	RMB800-1000
¥	葡萄酒价格：	$ $ $
	酒单酒款数：	247
	杯卖酒数：	16
¥	杯卖酒价格：	RMB135-245
	酒单撰写人：	Mr. Allen Wang
	电　话：	86 10 65237777
	营业时间：	17：30 - 23：00 （周一至周六）
		17：00 - 22：00 （周日）
	地　址：	北京市东城区金宝街 99 号丽晶酒店 2 层
@	网　址：	www.mortons.com

酒店的特色美式餐厅"东方路一号"重新定义了源自美国的现代烹调。餐厅环境亲切、温馨，弥漫着一种怀旧感，令人想起最初的"路易斯安娜"餐厅里那种美国南方宅第的室内装修风格。餐厅因供应世界各地的品牌葡萄酒而在京城首屈一指。客人们可在品酒师的推荐下品尝享用。餐厅的两个别致包间，是商务、家庭聚会的理想场所。

ONE EAST
东方路一号

美式

酒单大奖专家评审团之酒单点评：

这份酒单无疑是杰出的，它包括了一系列顶级香槟。同时，这里还罗列了当地生产商甄选的各个优质产区以及精品佳酿。丰富的选择总是令人格外愉悦。

The exceptional, mature cellar listing and a suite of fine, premium Champagnes, shines in a list that ably covers all bases from fine wine regions with a selection of established wine producers to some boutique offerings from well-chosen vintages. A broad list that offers lots of pleasure.

¥	人均消费：	RMB200
¥	葡萄酒价格：	$ $
	酒单酒款数：	233
	杯卖酒款：	10
¥	杯卖酒价格：	RMB50-94
	酒单撰写人：	Mr. Cina Houschyar
	电　　话：	86 10 58655030
	营业时间：	12：00-14：30, 18：00-22：30
	地　　址：	北京市朝阳区东三环北路 东方路一号希尔顿酒店二层
@	网　　址：	www.hilton.com.cn/beijing

Opera Bombana 是由米其林三星世界名厨 Umberto Bombana 在北京打造的全新餐厅。Opera Bombana 通过独特意大利风格的餐厅、新鲜烘焙面包、甜点、鸡尾酒和咖啡表达出名厨 Umberto Bombana 对于意大利美食和文化中基本元素的烹调热情。名厨 Bombana 利用当地能找到的最好食材为餐厅特意创造菜式，并由行政主厨 Marino d'Antonio 重新演绎。餐厅经理 Danny Allegretti 为客人精心挑选了选择广泛的葡萄酒。Opera Bombana 旨在呈现地道的意大利美食及轻松高雅的用餐体验，为北京的饕客带来口腹之欢。

OPERA BOMBANA

最佳新锐酒单

意式

酒单大奖专家评审团之酒单点评：

这份涵盖了意大利全国所有酒款的酒单附有一些经久不衰且独具特色的生产商。Vietti，La Spinetta 和 Col d'Orcia 都为这份有深度、有趣的酒单增添了亮色。这份酒单令人深刻而且具有原创精神。

A broad list of Italian wines that covers the whole country, with some exceptional back-vintage and feature producers included. Collections of Vietti, La Spinetta and Col d'Orcia, as examples, lend great depth and interest to this superb line-up. This is very impressive and original.

¥	人均消费：	RMB600
¥	葡萄酒价格：	$ $
🍷	杯卖酒数：	21
¥	杯卖酒价格：	RMB68-198
¥	开 瓶 费：	RMB400/ 餐厅购酒则可免开瓶费
👤	酒单撰写人：	Mr. Danny Allegretti
☎	电　　话：	86 10 56907177
🕐	营业时间：	12：00 - 14：30, 18：00 - 22：30
🏠	地　　址：	北京市朝阳区东大桥路 9 号 Parkview Green 芳草地地下二层 21 号单元
@	网　　址：	www.operabombana.com

记者俱乐部酒吧位于北京瑞吉酒店一层，紧邻阳光充沛的南走廊，酒吧内摆满了具有绅士俱乐部气息的真皮沙发和橡木墙裙，无不显露出与西绅总会的历史渊源。作为记者俱乐部的前身，西绅总会（北京俱乐部）在 1911 年初建于东交民巷，并于 1972 年迁至现址，更名为北京国际俱乐部。自兴建起，俱乐部一直作为驻京外交使节、新闻记者的专属聚会、娱乐和休闲场所。1997 年，北京瑞吉酒店建成开业后，俱乐部作为历史传承的重要组成部分被移至饭店内并定名为"记者俱乐部"。

PRESS CLUB BAR
记者俱乐部酒吧

酒单大奖专家评审团之酒单点评：

这份让人印象深刻的酒单涉及全球，从优质波尔多到顶级意大利，其中不乏来自澳大利亚和美国的佳酿。撇开葡萄酒不说，烈酒部分也同样出彩。可供选择的茶款也让人眼前一亮。多样化才是王道！

This is an impressive global list with a lot to like, from fine Bordeaux selections to grand wines of Italy with some excellent additions from Australia and USA. Wines aside, the spirits listings are deep and excellent, and don't miss the exceptional detail in the tea section! Diversity rules.

酒吧

¥	人均消费	RMB200
¥	葡萄酒价格	$ $
	酒单酒款数	207
♈	杯卖酒数	16
¥	杯卖酒价格	RMB85-165
♨	酒单撰写人	Mr. Ting Shan Chen
☎	电　话	86 10 64606688
⏰	营业时间	13：00 - 01：00
⌂	地　　址	北京市朝阳区建国门外大街 21 号 瑞吉酒店一层
@	网　址	www.stregis.com/beijing

法国米其林星级大厨 Alléno Yannick 创建的思餐厅于
2011 年 9 月 16 日在北京香格里拉饭店隆重开业。
寓意为 "Alléno Yannick 的典雅餐桌" 的思餐厅旨在
通过重新诠释传统的法国美食、以充满互动及轻
松有趣的用餐形式为宾客带来完美的用餐体验。
Yannick 善于通过对简单食材的巧妙运用，创作出
精美的创新法式经典菜肴。每道菜均由高品质、
新鲜时令的食材精心烹制而成。

S.T.A.Y.
思餐厅

法式

酒单大奖专家评审团之酒单点评：

你所能看到的 Roulot、Ramonet 和罗曼尼康帝还只是这
份史诗般酒单的开篇。在这段旅程中，来自法国、意
大利、澳大利亚的顶级酒款随处可见，而且产自偏远
地区的酒款又让酒单显得富有内涵且不枯燥。这是上上
之选。

The three 'Rs' here are Roulot, Ramonet and Romanee-Conti,
and that's just the start of this epic list. A journey through
pretty much every top-end, big name fine wine producer
from France, Italy, Australia and further afield makes for a very
exciting, very deep list. An exceptional selection.

¥	人均消费：	RMB800
¥	葡萄酒价格：	$ $ $
♟	酒单酒款数：	183
♟	杯卖酒数：	20
¥	杯卖酒价格：	RMB80-190
♟	酒单撰写人：	Mr Kun Zhou
☎	电　话：	86 10 68412211
⏱	营业时间：	11：30-14：00（周一至周五）
		11：30 - 15：00（周末）；17：30 - 22：00
🏠	地　址：	北京紫竹院路 29 号
		香格里拉饭店新阁一层
@	网　址：	www.shangri-la.com

刃扒房是一家屡获殊荣的牛排餐厅，可提供最嫩滑爽口的和牛牛排和时尚西式美食。客人们可以在烤架上烧烤上等牛排和海鲜产品，或尝试主厨 Mr. Zaller 的创意现代精致美食，所有美食均在开放式厨房一览无余。

THE CUT
刃扒房

西式

酒单大奖专家评审团之酒单点评：

尽管酒单上的顶级波尔多和香槟不在少数，核心却是多种多样的全球优质创新酒款。众多饱满的红葡萄酒适合搭配现代西餐，尤其是招牌的黑安古斯牛肉和纯种和牛。

While there is a fine selection of Bordeaux and Champagne, the heart of the list is an innovative and diverse spectrum of quality wines from around the world. Plenty of full-bodied reds to accompany the modern western menu, which specialises in quality black angus beef and pure-bred waygu.

¥	人均消费 :	RMB550
¥	葡萄酒价格 :	$ $ $
	酒单酒款数 :	160
	杯卖酒款数 :	11
¥	杯卖酒价格 :	RMB100-210
	酒单撰写人 :	Mr. Majeeth Faisal
	电　话 :	86 10 85117777
	营业时间 :	11：30 - 14：00（周一至周五）；18：00 - 22：30
	地　址 :	北京市朝阳区建国门外大街永安东里8号
@	网　址 :	www.fairmont.com/beijing

TRB 是一家现代欧洲菜系的西餐厅。餐厅致力于以最高标准的待客之道欢迎大家。餐厅的就餐区一度曾是用来生产电视机的厂房，北京的第一批黑白电视机就出自于此。TRB 的团队中有许多充满激情与敬业精神的厨师。随着客座世界名厨们的不断更迭和本土团队的不断创新，餐厅菜单也会经常更新，为大家带来新的惊喜。

TRB

最佳香槟酒单 — 中国大陆
最佳中国葡萄酒和烈酒酒单
中国北部地区最佳葡萄酒酒单
2014 中国酒单大奖 — 决赛入围名单

欧陆式

酒单大奖专家评审团之酒单点评：

这份酒单充分显示了对传统、佳酿的理解以及对新兴产区的关注。着重地选取了有机和生物动力法的酒款。酒单的长度和广度给人以深刻的印象，能称之为优秀的酒单一定是与众不同的。值得表扬。

Wow. Here's a list that shows understanding of traditional, fine wine and some of the more exciting, emerging wine regions, with an eye on the organic and biodynamic for good measure. Impressive in length and scope, an exceptional global list that dares to show some difference. Kudos.

¥	人均消费：	RMB600
♥	葡萄酒价格：	$ $
♦♡	酒单酒款数：	950
♥	杯卖酒数：	15
¥	杯卖酒价格：	RMB88-210
¥	开瓶费：	RMB350
♨	酒单撰写人：	Mr. Charles Sow
☎	电　话：	86 10 84002232
⏰	营业时间：	11：30 - 22：00
🏠	地　址：	北京市东城区沙滩北街 23 号
@	网　址：	www.trb-cn.com

拥有开放式厨房的香溢是一间新派餐厅，厨师们通过现场制作把每种饮食文化的特色淋漓尽致地演绎出来。除主就餐区域之外，餐厅还设有3间包房以及绿意盎然的户外庭院，可容纳超过200人同时用餐。餐厅提供了一个多样的就餐空间，无论是情侣甜蜜约会、家人欢聚抑或是团队聚餐，宾客都可以在香溢餐厅沐浴自然光，尽享美食与美酒。零点西餐以意大利菜为特色，其中最为有名的是特色菜——慢煮烤牛肉，这是搭配红酒的佳选。

ZEST
香溢

中式、意式、日式

酒单大奖专家评审团之酒单点评：

这份酒单有许多令人喜欢的地方，哪怕去掉＂列级庄＂的酒也能找到不少好酒。来自阿根廷、美国和意大利的众多酒款都非常诱人，车库酒商 Domaine Prieur Roch 也是不错的选择。酒单设计均衡又不失乐趣。

Impressive for many reasons, even beyond the 'Grand Cru Classe' section of the list that showcases some of the world great wines. Depth of wines from Argentina, USA and Italy are eye-catching, as are gems from cult producer Domaine Prieur Roch. Balanced and exciting list.

¥	人均消费：	RMB568
¥	葡萄酒价格：	$ $
	酒单酒款数：	300
	杯卖酒数：	15
¥	杯卖酒价格：	RMB120-180
¥	开 瓶 费：	RMB300
	酒单撰写人：	Mr. Mark Dong
	电　　话：	86 22 58578888
	营业时间：	06：30 - 22：00
	地　　址：	天津市和平区大沽北路167号
		丽思卡尔顿酒店一楼
@	网　　址：	www.ritzcarlton.cn

比萨高意大利餐厅给宾客带来意大利美味。行政总厨苏宝华先生的烹饪原则是
简单、真实。所有食材均为进口产品，蔬菜是厨房精心挑选的无公害有机食品。
在这里，宾客将品尝现制的比萨和面包、手工意大利面条、上好的海鲜和牛肉。

BISCOTTI ITALIAN RESTAURANT
比萨高意大利餐厅

意式

酒单大奖专家评审团之酒单点评：

这份赏心悦目的酒单将全球知名产区的佳酿收入囊
中。从波尔多一级庄到顶级香槟，还有从美国、南非
和中国搜罗的美酒。当然，意大利酒一定是菜单的最
佳搭配。

A cheerful list that shows best assets of the most well-known
wine regions of the world, from a couple of stunning First
Growths to premium Champagne and examples from USA,
South Africa and China for those seeking further interest.
Italian wines of course get time to shine with the food menu
too.

¥	葡萄酒价格：	S
🍷	酒单酒款数：	118
🍷	杯卖酒数：	22
¥	杯卖酒价格：	RMB58-128
👤	酒单撰写人：	Ms. Candy Ma
☎	电　话：	86 531 89816288
🏠	地　址：	济南市历下区泺源大街 66 号
		索菲特银座大饭店 2 层
@	网　址：	www.sofitel.com/2875

拥有 76 个座位的达芬奇餐厅以意大利建筑装饰风格为主线，辅以现代设计元素，将经典高雅与现代流行融合在一起。穿过砖墙装饰的走廊进入餐厅，你首先感受到的是高挑的空间，透过落地玻璃窗，都市风景尽收眼底。餐厅内的家具舒适豪华，处处营造浓厚的意大利氛围。餐厅选用纯正的橄榄油、谷物、蔬菜、香草、鱼和葡萄酒等新鲜原料，精心打造出堪称经典的意大利美食。

DA VINCI RESTAURANT
达芬奇意大利餐厅

酒单大奖专家评审团之酒单点评：

让人欣慰的是中国酒与华丽的勃艮第、美国酒和意大利酒同时出现。这不是一份冗长的酒单，精挑细选出可以与餐食搭配的酒款以及来自世界各地的佳酿。人人都能找到属于自己的那杯酒。

It's great to see wine from China getting some space on this list alongside luminaries from Burgundy, USA and Italy. It's not a long list, but it is well chosen and works very well with the cuisines and offers broad selection from around the world. Something for everyone.

意式

¥	人均消费：	RMB280
¥	葡萄酒价格：	$
	酒单酒款数：	118
	杯卖酒数：	19
	酒单撰写人：	Mr. Monica Lu
	电　话：	86 532 83883838
	营业时间：	11：30-14；30,17；30-22：00
	地　址：	青岛香格里拉大酒店盛世阁 3 楼
@	网　址：	www.shangri-la.com

东海 88 风味餐厅位于鲁商凯悦酒店一层，餐厅以时尚现代的手法将青岛悠久的渔业文化底蕴完美地体现在这间独具特色的风味餐厅，从木制的波浪形吊顶、星罗棋布的原木桌椅、现代感十足的鱼篓吊灯到门口整齐排列的大红锣鼓、鳞次栉比的茗茶瓷器以及古香古色的酒坛，让宾客领略到别有风味的青岛格调。特别设计的室外观海坐席能让醉人山海美景尽收眼底，全面升级客人们的美食体验。

DONGHAI 88
东海 88

最佳啤酒酒单

中式

酒单大奖专家评审团之酒单点评：

这份酒单集中了优秀的酒庄和出色的葡萄酒，以波尔多和勃艮第为主打。让人惊讶的是啤酒的部分，尤其是大名鼎鼎的修道士啤酒。烈酒的部分也让人印象深刻。这是一份富有创造力的酒单。

The wine list is very well appointed with fine producers and exceptional wines, with Bordeaux and Burgundy starring, but the real surprise is the exceptional beer listing, which shows impressively including excellent Trappist and Abbey brews. Spirits are also lengthy in listing. Creative list here.

❤	人均消费	RMB160
❤	葡萄酒价格：	$ $
❤	酒单酒款数：	114
❤	杯卖酒数：	8
❤	杯卖酒价格：	RMB55-130
❤	开 瓶 费：	RMB200
❤	酒单撰写人：	Mr. Michal Krauze
☎	电 话	86 532 86121234
⏱	营业时间：	11：30 - 14；30, 17：30 - 22：00
⌂	地 址：	青岛市东海东路 88 号鲁商凯悦酒店 1 层
@	网 址：	www.qingdao.regency.hyatt.com

坐落于二层的时尚海鲜烧烤餐厅"鲜"拥有世界顶级的食材,从澳洲的龙虾、牛肉到南太平洋的东星斑,专业的厨师团队严格挑选全球各地新鲜的有机食材,保证每次制作达到最佳水准,力求展现食物的自然原味,随时为宾客们精心烹烩豪华的味蕾盛宴。

C GILL AT CONRAD DALIAN
鲜餐厅

法式

酒单大奖专家评审团之酒单点评:

一份以"难以忘怀"酒作开始的酒单很难说会不受欢迎,更不用说随之而来的是顶级香槟、勃艮第、波尔多、澳大利亚和西班牙,除了这些昂贵的酒款,另一些新款和少见的酒也在可以选择的行列之中。这是一份考虑周全的酒单。

Hard to not like a list that starts with 'Unforgettable' wine selections then follows up with some of the grandest wines of Champagne, Burgundy, Bordeaux, Australia and Spain. Beyond the fancier wines are some thoughtful listings of emerging and lesser-known wines. Well balanced list.

💰	人均消费:	RMB400-500
🍷	葡萄酒价格:	$ $
🍾	酒单酒款数:	152
🍸	杯卖酒数:	85
🍷	杯卖酒价格:	RMB50-280
👤	酒单撰写人:	Mr. Marco Ma
📞	电 话:	86 411 86776666
🕐	营业时间:	11:30-14:30,17:30-22:00
🏠	地 址:	大连市中山区人民东路 31 号
@	网 址:	www.conradhotels.com.cn/dalian

　　“聚”餐厅为宾客提供完善的设施、舒适的环境，并且提供来自世界各地的最新菜品，同时“聚”餐厅的开放式厨房为客人们现场制作经典美食，还有来自世界各地的优良红酒供顾客选择；自助餐包含波士顿小龙虾、法式甜品、大连鲍、哈根达斯冰激凌。无限量畅饮啤酒饮料，让每一位光临“聚”餐厅的客人精彩无限、流连往返。

ELEMENTS
“聚”餐厅

法式

酒单大奖专家评审团之酒单点评：

作为长度中等的酒单，杯卖酒无疑是其强项，近30款的酒，覆盖面广，风格较多。这份酒单平易近人，很多芳香的白葡萄酒和酒体适中的红葡萄酒都适合佐餐。

For a medium-sized list it sure does flex its by-the-glass muscles, with just under 30 wines on offer and from across the whole spectrum of wine regions and styles of the list. The wine list feels friendly and accessible, with lots of aromatic whites and medium bodied reds friendly with the cuisine.

¥	人均消费	RMB208
¥	葡萄酒价格	$
酒	酒单酒款数	115
▼	杯卖酒数	25
👤	酒单撰写人	Mr. Frank G.P Louis
☎	电　　话	86 451 82336888
🕐	营业时间	11：30 - 14；00, 17；30 - 21；30
🏠	地　　址	哈尔滨市香坊区赣水路 68 号
@	网　　址	www.sofitel.com

绽放的睡莲，流淌的音乐，现代优雅的格调，宁静的餐前酒吧，巴黎餐厅处处洋溢着法式浪漫风情。精选上等食材，呈现艺术品般的精致菜品，并由专业侍酒师为宾客挑选环球精选美酒，带来最温暖难忘的用餐体验。

GRILL & WINE
巴黎餐厅

烧烤式

酒单大奖专家评审团之酒单点评：

在酒单上，新旧世界生产商所维持的平衡让人惊叹。既有来自澳大利亚、新西兰和南美的知名酒款，也有经典的欧洲酒，但更多是高性价比之作。尾页还有不错的中国烈酒以供选择。

Immediately appealing for it's balance of new and old world producers; a good showing of Australia, New Zealand and South American wines from notable wineries. Classics of Europe aren't ignored either, but more affordable options are on show. Good list of Chinese spirits to finish, too.

¥	人均消费：	RMB200-300
¥	葡萄酒价格：	$
	酒单酒款数：	131
♟	杯卖酒数：	17
¥	杯卖酒价格：	RMB50-198
♟	酒单撰写人：	Mr. Zi Wei Zhao
✆	电　　话：	86 351 8660000
⏱	营业时间：	11：30-14：30,17：30-22：30
⌂	地　　址：	太原市长风街 115-1
		凯宾斯基饭店二层
@	网　　址：	www.kempinski.com/zh-cn/taiyuan

Château Paradis Casseuil
凯萨天堂古堡

The vine of paradise from DBR (Lafite)
来自拉菲的天堂之藤

作为全城最高的酒店餐厅，佰鲜汇主要以海鲜为美食灵感，通过各国不同的烹饪技艺来呈现最精致的上品佳肴，每一道菜肴都是视觉与味觉完美结合的艺术品。另外，餐厅还提供来自世界各地的葡萄酒和香槟。由国际著名室内设计师梁志天打造的举目繁星的用膳空间亦将重新诠释"花城"商务社交和情侣约会的时尚聚所。

CATCH
佰鲜汇

西式和海鲜

酒单大奖专家评审团之酒单点评：

一些中肯的餐酒搭配建议足以表明酒款本身具有不错的质量。卓越的香槟精选、嘉伯乐和嘉雅的名家酒款以及对全球葡萄酒行业的远景展望都使之成为一份值得翻阅的酒单。

There's some great consideration in the food and wine matching suggestions which works as a good indication for the quality of wine to follow. Excellent Champagne selection, producers like Jaboulet and Gaja, and a broad global outlook on wine, make this an attractive list.

人均消费：	RMB588
葡萄酒价格：	$ $
杯卖酒数：	17
杯卖酒价格：	RMB88-158
酒单撰写人：	Mr. Jackie Zhang
电　话：	86 20 88833300
营业时间：	18：00 - 23：00
地　址：	广州市天河区珠江新城珠江西路 5 号四季酒店 100 层
网　址：	www.fourseasons.com/guangzhou/dining/restaurants/catch

Ebony 西餐厅提供上选肉品、空运新鲜海鲜和其他经典美食，宾客可以在午餐和晚餐时选择单点。在充满活力的餐厅中，宾客可一睹大厨们在设有法式烤炉、木制烤箱的开放式厨房中大展厨艺。服务生会将食物置于边桌上，为客人营造剧院般的用餐氛围。宾客也可选择在餐厅室外花园的草坪或树荫下用餐——白天在这里轻松享用午餐，晚上亦可在此感受月光下的宁静。

EBONY

中国南部地区最佳葡萄酒酒单

酒单大奖专家评审团之酒单点评：

任何一份以 96 年 Krug Clos du Ambonnay 或者 92 年香槟王珍藏桃红作开始的酒单一定具备很高的规格，其余的也都是各产区的优质酒庄。覆盖了全球主要产区的百科全书式的酒单令人印象深刻。

Any list that starts with bottles of '96 Krug Clos du Ambonnay or '92 Dom Pérignon Oenothèque Rosé is setting a certain high standard, and this menu continues with the hits from premier producers and regions. Encyclopaedic feel to this wine offering, across the wine-growing world. Very impressive.

烧烤式

🍴	人均消费：	RMB400
🍷	葡萄酒价格：	$ $ $
🍴	酒单酒款数：	341
🍷	杯卖酒数：	12
🍷	杯卖酒价格：	RMB120-480
👤	酒单撰写人：	Mr. Eric Blomeyer
📞	电　话：	86 20 38088884
🕐	营业时间：	18：00 - 22：00
🏠	地　址：	广州市天河区天河路 389 号 文华东方酒店 4 层
@	网　址：	www.mandarinoriental.com/guangzhou/ fine-dining/ebony

餐厅拥有新颖的开放式用餐环境，提供荔枝木无烟西式烧烤。这是一个精致又流光逸彩的时尚之地。餐厅坐落在酒店22楼，宾客可以通过落地式的窗墙向外看到生机勃勃的城市新中轴线，感受到城市新生的脉动。G回归最地道的西餐艺术，清爽的口感带来最原始的感动，让人在城央同样感受到浓浓的山情野趣，满足最单纯的美食渴望。

G RESTAURANT & BAR
G 烧烤餐厅

酒单大奖专家评审团之酒单点评：

如果你着眼于波尔多佳酿，那么这些被大篇幅地介绍、来自著名产区的美酒会让你欲罢不能。据说，澳大利亚、意大利、美国和勃艮第的精致酒款也有不错的评价。这是一张严谨的酒单。单一麦芽威士忌也可以试一试！

If you've got an eye for good Bordeaux, then you'll find yourself hard-pressed skipping the lengthy pages dedicated to reds of the famed region. That being said, cameos from benchmark Australian, Italian, USA and Burgundy wines also rate highly. A serious list. Don't miss the single malts either!

西式

¥	人均消费	RMB500-600
¥	葡萄酒价格	$ $
🍷	酒单酒款数	225
🍷	杯卖酒数	18
¥	杯卖酒价格	RMB88-280
¥	开瓶费	RMB250-500
👤	酒单撰写人	Mr. Cristiano Luk
☎	电话	86 20 83961234
🕐	营业时间	11：30-14：30，18：00-06：30
🏠	地址	广州市天河区珠江新城珠江西路12号22层
@	网址	www.guangzhou.grand.hyatt.com

意畔拥有典雅简约的异国风情、开放式的比萨壁炉，严守正宗地道的意大利菜式烹饪，不随波逐流、不落俗套，只为让食客愉悦且舒心地享受地道的意大利美味。在极具现代感而精致的装饰环境中，宾客可品尝到正宗地道的意大利美食。餐厅更设有 2 间私密专属的包房。

IL PONTE
意畔

意式

酒单大奖专家评审团之酒单点评：

布满著名酒款的酒单很容易就会被人记住，更别提那些被精心挑选出来的、覆盖了全球大部分优秀产区的酒。也就是说，酒单上列有许多顶级香槟、经典一级庄和著名波尔多。针对每款酒的描述让选择变得有趣。

A list that doesn't try too hard to impress with big names, but is crafted with attention to most of the world's great wine regions. That being said, a superb listing of Champagne and 'reserve' First Growth and notable Bordeaux is also on offer. Descriptions of each wine in the list is a delight.

¥	人均消费：	RMB190
¥	葡萄酒价格：	$ $
	酒单酒款数：	100
	杯卖酒数：	3
¥	杯卖酒价格：	RMB38-70
	酒单撰写人：	Mr. Arron Gwinnett
	电　话：	86 20 66833636
	营业时间：	11：30 - 14：30, 18：00 - 22：00
	地　址：	广州市天河区林和西横路 215 号
@	网　址：	www3.hilton.com/en/hotels

独具风格的意轩意大利餐厅位于广州富力丽思卡尔顿酒店三楼，由意大利名厨主理，汇集了从意大利精心挑选顶级的葡萄酒，带来精彩的正宗意式美食。特大型的酒窖、开放式的厨房以及与客人热情互动的大厨是餐厅亮丽的风景。

LIMONI ITALIAN RESTAURANT
意轩意大利餐厅

酒单大奖专家评审团之酒单点评：

这份酒单完全偏向意大利，利索地从 Prosecco 开始，接下来是顶级的托斯卡纳、皮埃蒙特和西西里酒，还有为数不多的其他国家酒款。窖藏精选红葡萄酒部分则为其增添了一些更为有趣的酒款。

The list leans heavily in the direction of Italy, starting with a neat selection of Prosecco and working up to more premium fare from Tuscany, Piedmont and Sicily, alongside some neat international wines. The Cellar Red Selection adds additional interest in this focussed list.

意式

人均消费：	RMB330
葡萄酒价格：	$ $
酒单酒款数：	189
杯卖酒数：	16
杯卖酒价格：	RMB98-380
酒单撰写人：	Mr. Kenny Persson
电　话：	86 20 38136688-8619
营业时间：	11：30-14：00（周一至周五）， 18：00-22：00（周一至周日）
地　址：	广州市天河区珠江新城兴安路3号
网　址：	www.ritzcarlton.com/en/Guangzhou

九号花园是一家以地中海美食为主的高级西餐厅。位于建设六马路的九号花园（总店）于 2007 年 12 月 9 日正式开业。九号花园以其自然、清新原味的烹调理念，提供创新多变的美食、浪漫优雅的地中海气氛，让食客在九号花园开始一次充满艺术的优质美食享受！

NO.9 GARDEN MEDITERRANEAN CUISINE
九号花园地中海餐厅

酒单大奖专家评审团之酒单点评：

侧重于意大利酒、西班牙酒的酒单与地中海式的菜系相得益彰。虽然酒款来自世界各地，但是里奥哈、托斯卡纳和皮埃蒙特的代表酒款仍为其增添光彩。香槟部分同样简洁明了。

With Mediterranean cuisine the theme of the food menu, it's great seeing such emphasis on Italian and Spanish wines. Though a global list, excellent wines from Rioja, Tuscany and Piedmont anchor the list, and show added class. Neat Champagne selection too.

地中海式

¥	人均消费：	RMB150
¥	葡萄酒价格：	$
♙	酒单酒款数：	196
♙	杯卖酒款数：	9
¥	杯卖酒价格：	RMB55-60
¥	开 瓶 费：	请向服务员咨询
♙	酒单撰写人：	Mr. Ned Cheung
☎	电 话：	86 20 83766197
⏱	营业时间：	12：00 - 02：00
⌂	地 址：	广州市越秀区建设六马路 9 号
@	网 址：	www.no9garden.com

坐拥深港美景的经典欧式餐厅“悦景”位于深圳君悦酒店37层，设计优雅且气氛怡人，训练有素的厨师团队为客人提供 à La Minute 餐饮体验，现场制作地道欧式美食，包括有口皆碑的进口高级牛扒，以欧式传统方法烤制，佐以自制的正宗酱汁，风味一绝，亦有优质海鲜供您随悉享用及品种繁多的佳酿供您搭配佳肴。浪漫典雅的用餐环境，温暖贴心的品质服务，每一个细节都极尽考究。

BELLE-VUE
悦景

欧式

酒单大奖专家评审团之酒单点评：

这份短小却精悍的酒单囊括众多大家之作。优质香槟打前阵，一系列顶级酒款随后而来。来自各个产区的约 20 款杯卖酒也让人兴奋。这是一份经过精挑细选的酒单。

This wine list packs in a lot for a shorter line-up; high quality Champagne leads the way, and a selection of premier wine regions follow. The by-the-glass selection is also inspiring, with just under 20 wines on offer, from fine wine producers around the winemaking world. A well-honed list

- 人均消费：RMB300 - 500
- 葡萄酒价格：$ $
- 酒单酒款数：131
- 杯卖酒数：17
- 电　　话：86 755 22187338
- 营业时间：18：00 - 22：00
- 地　　址：深圳市罗湖区宝安南路 1881 号
- 网　　址：www.shenzhen.grand.hyatt.com

时尚雅致的爵廊诠释着欧陆经典却不失现代奢华。精致的欧陆式美馔、城中规模最大的私藏酒窖、现代艺术品的点缀，使其成为发现时尚、宴客会友的理想之所。"爵廊"提供精品欧陆美味，诱人的西班牙小食带宾客感受来自地中海沿岸的美食灵感。典雅的二层奢华私人品酒区提供三百余款由深圳首位女侍酒师 Julia 精心挑选的葡萄佳酿，为美酒专家及初尝人士奉上恰到好处的餐酒选择。

DUKE'S
爵廊

西式

酒单大奖专家评审团之酒单点评：

这份严谨的酒单不仅提供了一部分世界顶级酒款，比如 DRC、Chateau Musar 年份酒以及优质澳大利亚酒，还有许多来自其他优秀产区的老酒和新酒。在杯卖酒中，你也能找到一些顶尖酒款。

A serious list that offers some of the world's greats, from Domaine de la Romanee Conti to vintage Chateau Musar and back to premium Australian wines, with an impressive selection of mature and young wines covering a great breadth of fine wine regions. By the glass showcases some premium wines too.

¥	葡萄酒价格：	$ $
	酒单酒款数：	393
	杯卖酒数：	21
¥	杯卖酒价格：	RMB65-195
	酒单撰写人：	Miss Julia Zhu
	电　话：	86 755 88289888
	营业时间：	18：00 - 01：00（周日至周四）
		18：00 - 02：00（周五及周六）
	地　址：	深圳市福田区深南大道 7888 号东海朗廷酒店三楼
@	网　址：	www.shenzhen.langhamhotels.com

香乐园的菜谱强调天然风味、注重食材的新鲜度、尽显地方风味。午餐和晚餐供应多款淮扬菜式，包括粤式烧腊、点心、滋补炖汤和时令海鲜。

SHANG GARDEN BAR
香乐园

淮扬菜式

¥	人均消费	RMB170
¥	葡萄酒价格	$
🍷	酒单酒款数	18
🍷	杯卖酒数	18
¥	杯卖酒价格	RMB70-190
👤	酒单撰写人	Mr. Michael Shin
☎	电　话	86 755 21513835
🕐	营业时间	11：30 - 14：30 , 17：30 - 22：30
🏠	地　址	深圳福田区益田路 4088 号
@	网　址	www.shangri-la.com

酒单大奖专家评审团之酒单点评：

这份短小的酒单不仅品类多样，而且十分有趣。其最大的吸引力在于每款都是杯卖酒。中国的麝香、南澳的 Viognier 和 Marsanne 的混合以及其他一些都是酒单撰写者独特品位的代表。

A very short list, but there's some diversity and interest nevertheless. Everything is available by the glass, which is also an attractive benefit of the listings. Muscat from China, viognier marsanne blend from South Australia and the uniqueness of some selections work in the list's favour.

烧烤餐厅坐落在美丽的深圳湾畔并面朝大海。从 70 个餐位上，客人都能观赏到无敌海景。用餐环境安静优雅。餐厅以提供用谷物饲养超过 300 天的澳大利亚安格斯牛的上等牛肉、6 到 8 级的雪花和牛为主，还有澳洲龙虾、美国波士顿龙虾和新鲜的澳洲生蚝，更有各国特色西式菜可供选择，尤其是从各地精选出来的芝士。精选自新旧世界的 377 款葡萄酒储藏在可容纳 1000 余酒瓶、进行全方位观赏的玻璃葡萄酒酒窖内。客人总能在酒窖里找到自己心仪的一款，或者专业的侍酒师也会帮助宾客进行餐酒搭配。

THE GRILL
烧烤餐厅

西式

酒单大奖专家评审团之酒单点评：

在这份酒单上，中国酒令人惊艳，不容忽视的还有产自澳大利亚、西班牙和美国的酒，当然波尔多酒也不例外地加了进来。但是，来自更多其它产区的酒款又让这份酒单显得完整且出类拔萃。香槟所占的篇幅也是足够长的。

A very impressive listing of wines from China is supported by wines from Australia, Spain and USA, though of course Bordeaux is exceptionally represented in this list too. But it's those other regions that complete the list and make it excel. Champagne is notably lengthy in listings too.

¥	人均消费	RMB500
¥	葡萄酒价格：	$ $ $
	酒单酒款数：	377
	杯卖酒数：	22
	杯卖酒价格：	RMB50-148
	酒单撰写人：	Mr. Joe Wen
	电　话：	86 755 21628888
	营业时间：	12：00 - 14：30,18：00 - 22：00
	地　址：	深圳市南山区望海路 1177 号
@	网　址：	www.shenzhenshekou.hilton.com

在园林阁的室内或是户外用餐，宾客均能欣赏到孔雀漫步于酒店花园的美景，感受充盈异国情调的氛围。园林阁独特的雕刻木屏风及优雅的鲜花摆设总能令人赏心悦目。优雅高脚烛台与蜡烛的搭配，更成为每日索菲特蜡烛仪式的必备元素，呈现索菲特最浪漫的法式艺术。园林阁提供地中海美食、蔬果、家禽、海鲜、谷物、豆类及意大利面食等的灵活搭配，让人食指大动。所有菜式均采用新鲜食材，沿用烘焙、烤、炸、烩等烹饪手法，为您呈现正宗地中海美食。精致牛排及芝士也备受欢迎。

GARDEN BISTRO
园林阁

西式

酒单大奖专家评审团之酒单点评：

这份西式菜单融合了各国经典，所以酒单也是如此，来自法国、意大利、南北美，泛亚太地区的酒款都有所涉及。如果你想要品尝一遍所有的酒款，那就试试套餐吧，一定会非常有趣！老年份的酒款也是这份酒单的特色之一。

The Western style menu covers a lot of ground. So too, does the wine list sprinkled with a smattering of French and Italian, North and South American and Australasian.For a quick dash around all of them look to the wine flights. What fun! Aged wines a feature here.

¥	葡萄酒价格：	$ $
	酒单酒款数：	212
	杯卖酒数：	47
¥	杯卖酒价格：	RMB50-115
	酒单撰写人：	Mr. Lip Chai Lim
	电　话：	86 769 22698888
	营业时间：	11：00 - 24：00
	地　址：	东莞市东城区迎宾路 8 号
@	网　址：	www.sofitel.com

"怡宴"地处中国十大文化古街区之首的福州三坊七巷营房里，贯通老城区的安泰河就流经"怡宴"的不远处，仿佛在悄悄地述说寻常巷陌间的陈年旧事。一本丰富的酒单是高级餐厅的标志之一。在"怡宴"，宾客可以从福州最佳酒单中挑选自己喜爱的美酒，餐厅侍酒师也会适时提供最直接的帮助和咨询。从意大利进口的 2 台分杯器为宾客增加了自主选择的机会。美酒与美食的巧妙融合是宾客的最佳选择。

EYAN
怡宴

法式、意式

酒单大奖专家评审团之酒单点评：

怡园酒庄旗下餐厅着眼于优质的中国葡萄酒。这是一个可以了解中国葡萄酒的好途径。不论是瓶装还是杯卖，可供选择的酒款众多，而且价格也十分合理。

The Grace Vineyard restaurant wine list highlights the quality produce of this established Chinese wine producer. A wonderful way to better know the wines of China. There's plenty of choose from either by the glass or bottle. Prices are reasonable.

💰	人均消费：	RMB220
🍷	葡萄酒价格：	$ $
🍾	酒单酒款数：	121
🍷	杯卖酒数：	14
💰	杯卖酒价格：	RMB38-88
💰	开 瓶 费：	RMB100
👤	酒单撰写人：	Mr. Sven Chen
☎	电　　话：	86 591 87760519
🕐	营业时间：	11：00 - 23：00
🏠	地　　址：	福州市鼓楼区营房里 18 号
@	网　　址：	www.grace-vineyard.com

顶级牛排和海鲜、西班牙餐前小食、经典拉丁鸡尾酒、古巴雪茄和品种丰富的葡萄藏酒等；"Q吧"环境温馨、舒适，具有怀旧气息和古巴风情，这里是下班小聚和夜晚社交的最佳场所；背景音乐、现场DJ表演以及开放式烧烤厨房提升餐厅就餐气氛.

QBA
Q 吧

拉丁式

酒单大奖专家评审团之酒单点评：

酒单虽小，但款款精选。创新型的酒款、中国葡萄酒以及新旧世界的代表之作也被罗列其中。在鸡尾酒部分，你还能找到具有厦门风格的调酒。

A small wine list it may be but there's some beaut finds within its pages including a creative wine flight, some up and coming Chinese wine producers and a tempting selection of Exceptional Wines from the New and Old Worlds. Check the cocktail list for a couple of Xiamen-inspired special offerings.

¥	人均消费	RMB300-400
¥	葡萄酒价格：	$ $
♨	酒单酒款数：	112
♚	杯卖酒数：	16
¥	杯卖酒价格：	RMB65-268
☺	酒单撰写人：	Mr. Dominic Ding
☎	电 话：	86 592 3378888
⏲	营业时间：	17：00 - 00：00（周一休）
⌂	地 址：	厦门市思明区仙岳路 398 号
@	网 址：	www.westin.com/xiamen

HELAN
MOUNTAIN
贺兰山

自然珍宝
揽誉全球

56个专业比赛　172个国际大奖

均3,000小时日照　　独特半沙质土壤　　黄河上游之水　　世界先进酿造技艺

至臻美味 共水相伴

意式生活

穿过酒架，进入主餐厅，简约巧妙的摆台让宾客对各式美食一目了然。精心搭配的黑色实木餐位、透明的玻璃幕墙让整个餐厅风格显得清新雅致，简约而不失华丽，细节之处彰显低调的奢华。香味西餐厅汇聚欧洲、亚洲及当地的传统经典美食。厨师团队不断探索中国美食的奥妙，并秉承西式经典烹饪元素，为宾客倾情奉上中西合璧的特色美食。自助餐包罗万象，包括琳琅满目的海鲜、口味纯正的欧式芝士和甜点，亚洲及东南亚风味美食应有尽有。

SPICES WESTERN RESTAURANT
香味西餐厅

西式

酒单大奖专家评审团之酒单点评：

以波尔多酒款作为后来者的标杆。新旧世界和谐地共存，从新西兰的清爽白到西班牙的经典红，还有精选的中国葡萄酒。套装酒款也值得一试。

From first page of wine there's finery - a list of excellent Bordeaux producers that sets a standard for what follows. There's a mesh of New and Old World wines, from vibrant whites of New Zealand to classic reds of Spain with some choice selections of local Chinese wine. Wine Flights are great too.

人均消费	：	RMB 108-238
葡萄酒价格	：	$ $
酒单酒款数	：	165
杯卖酒数	：	19
杯卖酒价格	：	RMB78-210
酒单撰写人	：	Mr. Remco Christiaan Vaatstra
电 话	：	86 23 68639999
营业时间	：	11：30 - 14：30，17：30 - 22：00
地 址	：	重庆市九龙坡区科园二路 137 号
网 址	：	www.sofitel-forebase-chongqing.com/6415

锦悦法餐厅位于成都锦江宾馆贵宾楼五层。面积约 2000 平方米的新餐厅拥有 90 个餐位，还有 400 平米的两处花园露台。宾客可以在露天花园里观赏到四季美景的同时，享用精致可口的法式下午茶点，领略法国饮食文化。这是一个以米其林星级餐厅标准设计的、成都锦江宾馆与梅斯城堡酒店合作打造的纯法式餐厅。

JINYUE FRENCH RESTAURANT
锦悦法餐厅

中国西部地区最佳葡萄酒酒单

法式

酒单大奖专家评审团之酒单点评：

法国酒的深度本来就特别吸引人，更不用说婷芭克，莎普蒂尔和杜鲁安那些高品质的酒款。波尔多酒款已然不错，但是罗讷河谷、勃艮第和卢瓦河也不容小觑。

Particularly appealing for its depth of French wine, but enhanced by the feature producers like Trimbach, Chapoutier and Drouhin getting some extra attention and offering their upper tiers of wines. Of course the Bordeaux listings are impressive, but Rhone, Burgundy and Loire hold their own too.

人均消费：	RMB1000
葡萄酒价格：	$ $
酒单酒款数：	90
杯卖酒款数：	9
杯卖酒价格：	RMB88-288
酒单撰写人：	Mr. Ailing Wang
电　话：	86 28 85506199
营业时间：	11：00 - 21：30
地　址：	成都市锦江宾馆贵宾楼 5 楼
网　址：	www.jjhotel.com/EN/Default.aspx

丽轩中餐厅的设计灵感来自两千多年的古蜀文明。因秉承"芙蓉古都"为设计理念，随处可见的蜀锦装饰、缤纷花朵将摩登时尚的餐厅点缀出成都气息。餐厅主打精品粤菜，辅以特色川菜。主厨梁师傅亲手设计的丽轩中餐厅菜单，从开胃冷菜到广式烧味，生猛海鲜到美味汤羹，可口主食到精致点心，素食主义到新派川菜，花胶燕窝到鲍鱼海参，各式美味，一应俱全。

LI XUAN CHINESE RESTAURANT
丽轩中餐厅

粤式川式

酒单大奖专家评审团之酒单点评：

行家们对于整齐罗列的波尔多酒一定喜闻乐见。这份酒单覆盖全球，精选出最优的产区和知名生产商。精挑细选的意大利酒也值得关注。酒单上可以尝试的酒款非常多。

An impressive list of Bordeaux neatly organised for connoisseurs is the highlight of a list that works a global line-up, selected for best winegrowing regions and notable producers from each. Italian wines are also well-selected and worthy of attention. Lots to drink here.

¥	人均消费：	RMB300-600
¥	葡萄酒价格：	$
	酒单酒款数：	279
	杯卖酒款数：	21
¥	杯卖酒价格：	RMB80-180
	酒单撰写人：	Mr. Luke Liu
	电　话：	86 28 83588888
	营业时间：	11：30 - 14：30, 17：30 - 22：30
	地　址：	成都市青羊区顺城大街 269 号 丽思卡尔顿酒店 26 层
@	网　址：	www.ritzcarlton.com/en/Properties/ Chengdu

秀餐厅环境优美、视野开阔，并配有落地窗，全天候地为宾客供应丰盛多样的美食，包括早餐、午餐和晚餐。在晚餐时段，客人们可享用行政总厨特别创制的开胃小菜和甜点自助餐以及包括红烧海鲜和牦牛肉三吃在内的每日精选菜品。餐厅设计精美，拥有高天花板，采用暖色木材和白色墙面装饰，处处流露出充满活力的迷人色彩。墙壁上绘有各种藏式图案，包括牦牛在白雪皑皑的喜马拉雅山上奔跑的景象。餐厅可容纳 80 名客人轻松就餐，并设有一间 10 人座席的私人包房。

SOCIAL RESTAURANT
秀餐厅

酒单大奖专家评审团之酒单点评：

这会是西藏最好的酒单吗？像意大利的嘉雅和法国奥比昂这样大名鼎鼎的酒庄也都榜上有名，还有众多优质酒款可供选择，中国酒也在榜单上。

Could this be the best wine list in Tibet? Certainly shows some depth with big name producers like Italy's Gaja and Chateau Haut Brion featured. Lots to choose from in terms of premium wines, but a neat selection of Chinese wines are found too.

西式

¥	葡萄酒价格：	＄ ＄
🍴	酒单酒款数：	80
🍷	杯卖酒款数：	1
👤	酒单撰写人：	Mr. Allen Wang
☎	电　话：	86 891 6808888
🕐	营业时间：	06：30 - 23：00
🏠	地　址：	西藏拉萨江苏路 22 号
@	网　址：	www.stregis.com/lhasa

类人首®

黄金葡园 阳光美酒

品　牌：类人首金牌橡木桶窖藏干红葡萄酒

类　型：干　红

品　种：赤霞珠、梅洛

产　地：宁夏贺兰山东麓玉泉营

酒精度：13.5%vol

净含量：750ml

年　份：2009年

酒评：淡淡的烤面包与奶油香气，与甘草，肉桂相互交织，成熟的黑色浆果与橡木香气结合的恰到好处，单宁细腻、雅致，酒体平衡且丰满，酸度中强后段显现，层次感鲜明令人回味悠长。

配餐：红葡萄酒中的单宁能与红肉中丰富的蛋白质相结合，让肉质更加鲜嫩多汁，入口留香。

中国·宁夏产区
www.leirenshou.com

宁夏类人首葡萄酒庄兴建于2002年，是一家集葡萄种植、生产、销售于一体的农业产业化优秀龙头企业。酒庄位于宁夏贺兰山东麓葡萄原产地域核心地带，先后两次花费巨资从法国、澳大利亚引进先进成熟的酿酒技术，并长期聘请著名专家进行指导，为酒庄不断提升产品品质奠定坚实的技术基础。2013年，酒庄成为中国首批十大列级酒庄之一。

Chateau Leirenshou Ningxia was founded in year 2002. It is an industrialized agricultural corporate champion, which combines wine grapes growing, wine producing and sales. It is located at the east foot of Helan Mountain, the central area of geographical indications and designations of origin for wines. Chateau Leirenshou invested costly twice for the advanced brewing techniques and equipment from France and Australia, and also continuously brings in famous wine experts to advise on the improvement of the wine quality, which ensures the solid foundation of techniques for making high quality wine. Thanks to that, Ch?teau Leirenshou was classified and designated as one of the first ten grand crus in Ningxia.

宁夏类人首葡萄酒业有限公司
地址：宁夏银川市永宁县玉泉营农场
电话：0951-8450111
网址：www.leirenshou.com

扫一扫，关注类人首公众平台

WATCH THE BACKSTAGE ON
WWW.CANTINEFERRARI.IT
FERRARI
BRUT
FERRARI
BRUT
THE ITALIAN ART OF LIVING
Venezia, Piazza San Marco ore 4:54
FERRARI
TRENTO 1902

香港   116 - 142

酒吧每月都会更新葡萄酒单，其中的杯卖酒部分涵盖意大利的每个产区。同时，这里还会提供以时令食材进行简单烹饪的料理。

121 BC

  最佳酒吧酒单

意式

酒单大奖专家评审团之酒单点评：

这是一份精炼、性价比高的酒单。121BC 向大家展示着香港未来的餐厅风格——规模绝不是一切。在赞赏知名的意大利酒同时，我们也不要忘记那些有趣且罕为人知的杯卖酒款。

Small, modest in price and aspirations, 121 BC just might be showing the way for a future in Hong Kong dining where size isn't everything. We applaud the 100 per cent focus on Italian wines and the number of interesting wines by the glass from some of the quieter, smaller producers going.

- ¥ 人均消费： HKD120
- 葡萄酒价格： $ $
- 杯卖酒数： 20
- ¥ 杯卖酒价格： HKD60-125
- 酒单撰写人： Mr. Simone Sammuri
- 电 话： 852 23950200
- 营业时间： 17：00 - 00：00（周一、周日休）
- 地 址： 香港中环卑利街 42-44 号
- @ 网 址： www.121bc.com.hk

Mr. Antonio Bombini

8½ Otto e Mezzo BOMBANA Hong Kong 是由米其林三星世界名厨 Umberto Bombana 开设及主理的高级意大利餐厅。餐厅位于中环历山大厦的二楼，占地约 4700 平方尺。在 Bombana 的亲自监督下，日本著名设计工作室 Design Post 操刀室内设计。整间餐厅的风格以简约优雅为主。当进入主餐厅时，切勿错过那独特的陈年老窖，这里面收藏着 Bombana 的珍藏——顶级意大利火腿 Pata Negra、Cinta Senese 以及经他严选出来的意大利芝士、鱼子酱、松露和橄榄油等。自 2011 年开始，8½ Otto e Mezzo BOMBANA Hong Kong 就被《米其林指南 香港 澳门》连续三年评审为三星食府，是意大利境外第一家获米其林三星荣誉的意式食府。

8½ OTTO E MEZZO BOMBANA HONG KONG

意式

酒单大奖专家评审团之酒单点评：

在这份令人热血沸腾的酒单上，意大利和法国你追我赶。但是意大利以更多的皮埃蒙特和托斯卡纳精选酒款而胜出。杯卖酒单引人入胜，此外还有众多半瓶和大瓶装可供选择。

The wines of Italy play tag with those of France throughout this enthusiastic wine list but the Italians win outright with a greater depth of selections led by Piedmonte and Tuscany. Wines by the glass are particularly appealing supported by a thorough half bottle/magnums collection.

¥	人均消费：	HKD500-1400
¥	葡萄酒价格：	$ $ $
♟	酒单酒款数：	687
♟	杯卖酒数：	31
¥	杯卖酒价格：	HKD90-440
♟	酒单撰写人：	Mr. Antonio Bombini
☎	电　　话：	852 25378859
◷	营业时间：	12：00 - 14：00，18：30 - 22：30
⌂	地　　址：	香港中环遮打道 18 号
		历山大厦 202 号店
@	网　　址：	www.ottoemezzobombana.com

集餐厅、酒吧和会所于一身的 Alfie's 展示地道的英式风格，让顾客从都市中逃离，来到这个随意、亲密、精致的环境中享用美食美酒、鸡尾酒和单一麦芽威士忌。自 2010 年 4 月开业以来，Alfie's 成为宾客享用丰盛的早午餐、下午茶和晚餐的去处。Alfie's 集团行政主厨 Rolad Levy Schuller 将其对英伦生活的理解带入 Alfie's，欢迎宾客前来品尝典型的英式早餐，比如香肠、土豆泥或者太妃甜饼，或者可以品尝具有地中海风情的无谷蛋白有机食物，比如慢煮海鳟、藜麦饭或者栗子扁面条。

ALFIE'S

酒单大奖专家评审团之酒单点评：

这份小酒单是在 Sarment 葡萄酒管理集团的协助下而制作完成。这里列有澳大利亚的 Garagiste、法国的 Jacques Picard 和一组一级园。不仅酒款的价格合适，而且葡萄酒爱好者也会从中获得新的发现。

This smart wine list is compiled with assistance from the Sarment wine management group and contains some real finds such as Garagiste (Aus), Jacques Picard (Fr) as well as a smashing grouping of Premier Crus. Prices are fair and there's plenty of new discovery for wine lovers.

英式

¥	人均消费:	HKD300-500
¥	葡萄酒价格:	$ $
	酒单酒款数:	172
	杯卖酒数:	9
¥	杯卖酒价格:	HKD90-150
¥	开瓶费:	HKD250
	电　话:	852 25304422
	营业时间:	07：00-24：00
	地　　址:	香港遮打道6-14A号太子大厦
		中环遮打道10号 M18-19号
@	网　址:	www.dunhill.com/the-homes/hong-kong

Aqua Roma/Aqua Tokyo 再一次重新定义了其超时尚的装饰、迷人的海港和城市景观，创新的菜单结合了最好的意大利料理和日本料理，在这里，宾客将会得到一个极好的用餐体验。Aqua Roma/Aqua Tokyo 侧重于传统的意大利美食与现代气息。

AQUA ROMA/AQUA TOKYO

意式、日式

酒单大奖专家评审团之酒单点评：

将意大利美食与美酒和日本美食与美酒结合在一起？虽然这会很困难，但是 Aqua Roma 做到了——更多地将酒款搭配意大利菜。这是一份全面且有可看性的意大利酒单，最后还附有一份简短精悍的清酒单。

Italian and Japanese food and wine together? That's a hard act to follow with wine but Aqua Roma gives the idea its best shot with a wine list angled mainly towards the former. Some nice, all-round quality Italian wines can be found. A small but tidy listing of sake follows.

¥	人均消费：	HKD400-800
¥	葡萄酒价格：	$ $ $
🍷	杯卖酒数：	22
¥	杯卖酒价格：	HKD98-138
¥	开瓶费：	HKD650
👤	酒单撰写人：	Mr. Bartlomiej Szyniec
☎	电　话：	852 34272288
🕐	营业时间：	12：00 - 15：00,18：00 - 23：00
🏠	地　址：	香港九龙尖沙咀北京道一号二十九及三十楼
@	网　址：	www.aqua.com.hk

Catalunya 是一家由正宗的加泰罗尼亚食谱衍生而来的现代西班牙餐厅。这家餐厅拥有众多西班牙葡萄酒、地中海人民的好客、专业而友好的服务以及时下最流行的鸡尾酒。厨师队伍来自全球顶尖的西班牙餐厅，比如 El Bulli、El Celler de Can Roca。餐厅能容纳 140 人，设有 2 个主要用餐区域、1 个包间和一间鸡尾酒会所。多感官的体验、传统的当地食材以及西班牙的美食让宾客不虚此行。

CATALUNYA

西班牙式

酒单大奖专家评审团之酒单点评：

加泰罗尼亚，起泡酒"卡瓦"的故乡。这份酒单内含许多西班牙起泡酒和众多西班牙贵族酒。对于刚开始喝西班牙酒的人来说，杯卖酒是首选，款款物美价廉。这份朴实的酒单对其他产区也有所涉猎，并提供了一些奇珍异宝。

Ah, Catalunya . . . the home of Cava. Expect to drink Spanish sparkling and a whole lot of Spanish blue bloods here. Look no further than wines by the glass for a good introduction to Spain at fair prices. This unpretentious all-rounder looks outside Spain too, offering the odd gem.

¥	葡萄酒价格：	$ $
	酒单酒款数：	400
	杯卖酒数：	10
¥	杯卖酒价格：	HKD88-158
	酒单撰写人：	Mr. Miquel Sabrià
	电　话：	852 28667900
	地　址：	香港湾仔爱群道 32 号 Morrison Hill 爱群商业大厦 G / F
@	网　址：	www.catalunya.hk

La Table de Patrick 的设计让人想起了充满现代和时尚气息的巴来公寓。墙壁的设计以冷灰色的色调搭配金色的手绘壁纸。至于 La Table de Patrick 餐厅的招牌菜，有鹅肝三重奏、Chateaubriand 黑安格斯配烤土豆和羊乳酪酱、鲈鱼鱼柳、扇贝和大虾鱼汤等菜式。

LA TABLE DE PATRICK

（原名 Chez Patrick Restaurant)

法式

酒单大奖专家评审团之酒单点评：

尽管这份非常优秀的小型酒单内含高性价比且有趣的 75 款酒，但其重点仍是法国酒，更有诸如 Meo Camuzet、Jadot 和 Certan de May 这些著名酒商的物超所值的酒款。老酒、新酒任君挑选，你很容易就能找到中意的酒款。

A most charming small wine list of just 75 wines full of interest and fantastic value for money.It remains focussed on French wines with some delicious medium priced examples from quality producers like Meo Camuzet, Jadot and Certan de May. Aged wines mingle with fresh youngsters. Lots to like here.

¥	人均消费	HKD800
¥	葡萄酒价格：	$ $
	酒单酒款数：	75
♟	杯卖酒数：	10
¥	杯卖酒价格：	HKD80-180
¥	开瓶费：	HKD250
♟	酒单撰写人：	Mr. Patrick Goubier
☎	电　话：	852 25411401
⏲	营业时间：	12：00 - 15：00, 19：00 - 23：00 (周日休)
⌂	地　　址：	香港环阁麟街 37-43 号祥兴商业大厦电梯 6 楼
@	网　　址：	www.chezpatrick.hk

Mr. Alan Sun

餐厅展示了当代粤菜的用餐体验，包括大厨的精湛手艺及高级食材的选用。国金轩的著名单点菜谱、午市以及晚市的时令套餐更将美食烹调幻化成一种艺术，表达了厨师对不同季节性的食材和口味的遵循。国金轩之其中一间贵宾房以多达 350 种葡萄酒为点缀布置，另备有专人侍酒服务，让食客品尝来自世界各地的极品佳酿。

CUISINE CUISINE
国金轩

粤式

酒单大奖专家评审团之酒单点评：

一份巧妙的粤菜单与满是耳熟能详的酒款的酒单相得益彰。这份酒单一定能让喜欢新旧世界的传统酒款的爱好者蠢蠢欲动。不过令人遗憾的是，中国葡萄酒还不在可选择范围内。

A smart Cantonese food menu is well supported by a world wine listing full of familiar wine names. The list will be reassuring to those who love the iconic producers of both the New and Old Worlds. Sadly, no Chinese wine producers have yet come on board.

¥	人均消费	HKD250-500
¥	葡萄酒价格	$ $
♟	酒单酒款数	365
♟	杯卖酒数	12
¥	杯卖酒价格	HKD95-2125
¥	开 瓶 费	HKD350
☺	酒单撰写人	Mr. Alan Sun
☎	电 话	852 23155222
⏲	营业时间	11；30 - 22；30（周一至周六）
		10；30 - 22；30（周日及公众假期）
⌂	地 址	香港九龙尖沙咀弥敦道 118 号
		The Mira Hong Kong 3 楼
@	网 址	www.themirahotel.com

Mr. Kevin Yung

Flint Grill & Bar 位于世界知名的香港 JW 万豪酒店内，着重强调食材的新鲜品质、厨师的精湛手艺以及团队的无限创意。餐厅洋溢摩登工业风格，一众美食爱好者能在亲切舒适的氛围中，享用完美烹调而成的顶级肉扒、新鲜海鲜等特色美馔，精心搭配美酒佳酿及创意无限的招牌鸡尾酒，同时近距离欣赏烹饪过程。大厨选用世界各地的新鲜食材，悉心地为宾客缔造创新互动餐饮概念。

FLINT GRILL & BAR

烧烤式

酒单大奖专家评审团之酒单点评：

Flint Grill & Bar 提供了 146 个席位和 146 款酒款。分别来自于新旧世界的不同酒款在酒单所占的比例均衡，唯一有所侧重的是现在流行的勃艮第。这里多是近几年的酒款。可以试试招牌鸡尾酒。

Flint Grill & Bari boasts 146 seats and 146 wines. Nice synergy! The wine list gives equal time to wine styles from the Old and New Worlds with a particularly envy-worthy grouping of smart Burgundies. Vintages tend to be on the fresher side. Try the Signature Cocktails to start.

¥	人均消费：	HKD400
¥	葡萄酒价格：	$ $
🍷	酒单酒款数：	146
🍷	杯卖酒数：	19
¥	杯卖酒价格：	HKD85-388
¥	开瓶费：	HKD400
👤	酒单撰写人：	Mr. Kevin Yung
☎	电　话：	852 28108366
🕐	营业时间：	12：00-14：30,18：00-22：30
🏠	地　址：	香港金钟道 88 号香港 JW 万豪酒店 5 楼
@	网　址：	www.jwmarriotthongkong.com/dining

深受本地及海外饕客喜爱的金叶庭向来以精致粤菜享负盛名。现已被《米其林指南 香港 澳门 2014》评为"一星食府"。金叶庭的装潢古典瑰丽，缀以传统柚木及檀木家具及古董摆设，营造出华贵醉人的气氛。午餐及晚餐时段的自选菜谱包含一系列正宗广东佳肴，在星期六、日及公众假期则另设点心早餐。

GOLDEN LEAF
金叶庭

粤式

酒单大奖专家评审团之酒单点评：

尽管酒单覆盖面广，但是大部分的爱好者还是会容易沦陷在法国酒和意大利酒部分。来自皮埃蒙特、托斯卡纳的垂直年份酒和罗讷河谷的酒都备受好评。半瓶装绝对值得考虑一下。

While the list is enthusiastically international in scope, most wine lovers will find it hard to take their eyes off the French and the Italians. The Rhone Valley wines and the verticals of reds from Piedmont and Tuscany are highly appealing. Half bottles are worth a serious consideration.

¥	人均消费	HKD500
¥	葡萄酒价格	$ $ $
	酒单酒款数	530
	杯卖酒数	12
¥	杯卖酒价格	HKD65-198
¥	开瓶费	HKD500
	酒单撰写人	Mr. Lee Watson
	电　话	852 28225777
	营业时间	11：30 - 15：00，18：00 - 23：00
	地　址	香港金钟道 88 号太古广场香港港丽酒店大堂底座
@	网　址	www.conraddining.com

于 2013 年开业的意大利餐厅及酒吧 Il Milione Bar & Ristorante Italiano 把意大利美食的精髓带到香港。餐厅自开业以来已赢得 "Hong Kong Top 10 Wine Pairing Restaurant Award"、"Hong Kong Best Restaurant" 以及 "Wine By The Glass Restaurant Awards 2014" 等多项殊荣，并于 2014 年获得 "米其林一星食府" 荣誉。餐厅除了为顾客呈献一系列特色意国美食，部分菜色还充满意大利翁布里亚风味。餐厅的名字取自著名的《马可·波罗游记》，寓意餐厅致力于将意大利传统烹饪经验带到其他地方，就如 13 世纪引领文化和贸易交流的先驱一样。

IL MILIONE BAR & RISTORANTE ITALIANO

意式

酒单大奖专家评审团之酒单点评：

去年开张的 Il Milione 绝对是意大利酒爱好者的饕餮之地。翁布里亚菜系最好配杯翁布里亚酒，Sagrantino 红葡萄酒看上去更不错。用意大利酒盛情款待，还有比托斯卡纳和维内托更好的选择？哪怕吃多了也得来杯甜酒。

Opened last year, Il Milione bursts with Italian gusto. With an emphasis on the food of Umbria we suggest you consider an Umbrian wine partner, the sagrantino reds look particularly smart. Italian wines are done proud, no better than the Tuscany and Veneto listings. The dessert wines are to die for.

¥	人均消费	HKD1,000-1,300
¥	葡萄酒价格	$ $
	酒单酒款数	380
	杯卖酒数	15
¥	杯卖酒价格	HKD100-280
¥	开瓶费	HKD500
	酒单撰写人	Mr. Bojan Radulovic
	电　话	852 24811120
	营业时间	12：00 - 24：00
	地　址	香港中环夏悫道 10 号和记大厦地下 16-21 号铺
@	网　址	www.il-milione.com

冈田和生日本餐厅主打极尽精致及讲究的日式料理——
怀石料理。餐厅设计别具一格，中央的开放式厨房更通
过灯光效果突显大厨的厨艺与功架。

在奖项方面，餐厅除获得《米其林指南 香港 澳门》2013
及 2014 年度"上佳的餐厅"推介外，其他奖项包括"*Hong
Kong Tatler*"杂志之 2013 及 2014 年度"香港及澳门最
佳食府"、"2014 春季香港餐厅周"之"最佳餐单"大
奖。

KAZUO OKADA
冈田和生

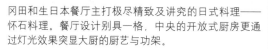

日式

酒单大奖专家评审团之酒单点评：

只有早点到达 Kazuo Okada，你才能仔细观摩那份绝佳
的酒单。你不仅会一饱眼福，还可能口水直流。来自
法国和意大利的精选酒，尤其是香槟，将带领你来到
世界的另一端。

Arrive at Kazuo Okada early to give yourself time to feast
your eyes over this extraordinary international wine list. The
drool factor is high. The exhaustive selection of French and
Italian wines, particularly Champagne, leads onto to an equally
thorough approach to the rest of the world.

人均消费：	HKD500-1200
葡萄酒价格：	$ $ $
酒单酒款数：	1903
杯卖酒数：	22
杯卖酒价格：	HKD55-480
开 瓶 费：	HKD300
酒单撰写人：	Mr. Akihiko Nosaka
电 话：	852 37462722
营业时间：	12：00-14：30（周末）
	18：00-23：00（周二至周日）
地 址：	香港九龙红磡环海街 11 号海名轩 5 楼
网 址：	www.kodining.com

由著名米其林二星名厨 Philippe Leveille 开设，位于中环 L.Place 的意大利餐厅 L'altro 以意大利文 l'altro 命名。顾名思义，旨在通过提供另类选择，为食客带来不一样的体验。法籍行政总厨 Leveille 擅长糅合法式烹调技巧于传统地道意式佳肴，曾被具有影响力之意大利杂志 "*Grande Cucina*" 选为在过去十年里最具代表性之厨师。他亲驻新店，与才华横溢的意大利籍主厨 Mauro Zacchetti 一同打造高级意式佳肴。

L'ALTRO

意式

酒单大奖专家评审团之酒单点评：

L'altro 的意大利菜可以搭配酒单上众多意大利酒，但选择并不局限于此。更多精美的酒款等着你来选择，97 年巴罗洛以及 82 年一级庄都在选择之列。杯卖酒或者半瓶装也是不错的选择。

A solid list concentrating on Italian wines to match L'altro's rich Italian cuisine but also offering so much more. There's room to splurge: '97 Barolos, '82 First Growths are mouth-watering propositions or there's always a serious selection of glass and half bottles to fall back on.

¥ 人均消费：HKD300-1,000
¥ 葡萄酒价格：$ $ $
杯卖酒数：21
¥ 杯卖酒价格：HKD118-248
酒单撰写人：Mr. Derek Li
电　话：852 25559100
营业时间：11：30 - 14：30，18：30 - 22：30
地　址：香港中皇后大道中
　　　　　139 L.Place 10 楼
@ 网　址：www.laltro.hk

Eric Yau

Terence Wong

L'atelier de Joël Robuchon 于 2006 年在香港开业，并于 2012 至 2014 年连续三年荣获《米其林指南 香港 澳门》三星评级。餐厅分为两个部分：L'atelier 及 Le Jardin。L'atelier 的设计为一个围绕着开放式厨房的 U 形吧台，让顾客可以亲睹主厨由烹调至摆放食物上桌的每一步骤。L'Atelier 提供多种法国传统菜式，并以创新的食物呈现方式，为顾客带来味觉和视觉的双重享受。Le Jardin 的室内设计优雅，顾客可以一边欣赏露天茶座的景色，一边品尝经典的法国菜肴，体验时尚的餐喝享受。

L'ATELIER DE JOËL ROBUCHON

中国年度最佳葡萄酒酒单 — 香港、澳门及台湾地区
香港地区最佳葡萄酒酒单
最佳独立餐厅酒单

法式

酒单大奖专家评审团之酒单点评：

尽管这里只有新葡京酒窖的部分酒款，那也是星光熠熠、名家云集。全球知名的众多年份酒款，并附有酒评家的分数作为参考。醉人的经典法国酒以及新世界和意大利的众多酒款都出现在这份酒单上。另有 17 款优质杯卖酒可以一试。

A glittering subset of the great cellar found at the Grand Lisboa Hotel. Multiple vintages of the world's best wines with critics' scores listed as a guide. There's a heady list of French classic plus numerous new world and Italian reds. A sensational wine by-the-glass selection – 17 in total.

¥	人均消费	HKD478-1880
¥	葡萄酒价格	$ $ $
	酒单酒款数	3262
	杯卖酒数	11
¥	杯卖酒价格	HKD210-560
¥	开瓶费	禁止自带酒水
	酒单撰写人	Mr. Terence Wong & Mr. Eric Yau
	电 话	852 21669000
	营业时间	12：00-14：30,18：30-22：30
	地 址	香港中环皇后大道中 15 号 置地广场 4 楼 401 号铺
@	网 址	www.robuchon.hk

Messina Il Ristorante 以意大利西西里的一个城市命名，为食客呈献意大利南部美馔。大厨擅长把法式烹调技巧融入意大利佳肴中，招牌菜式包括薄切生吞拿鱼片及意式烤脆皮猪。餐厅已获得《米其林指南 香港 澳门 2013》"上佳的餐厅"推介，其他奖项包括 *Hong Kong Tatler* 杂志之 2013 及 2014 年度"香港及澳门最佳食府"、"第四届香港餐厅周"之"最佳餐厅"大奖 (2013)、"2014 春季香港餐厅周"之"最受欢迎餐厅"大奖、Ospitalia Italiana 优质及正宗意大利餐厅验证。

MESSINA IL RISTORANTE

意式

酒单大奖专家评审团之酒单点评：

作为"玉蕾"餐厅和日本餐厅 Kazuo Okada 的姊妹餐厅，这里也有一份相同酒款的酒单，但配菜只有西西里式菜肴。意大利酒部分提供了多样的选择，其中就有西西里酒。而开胃酒也不再局限于优质香槟。

A sister wine list to Yu Lei restaurant and Kazuo Okada Japanese restaurant sharing the same wines but here, they are asked to match Sicilian cooking. The Italian section offers plenty of choice, including Sicilian wines. For your aperitif you can't go further than the exceptional Champagne list.

¥	人均消费：	HKD300-1000
¥	葡萄酒价格：	$ $ $
	酒单酒款数：	1903
	杯卖酒数：	22
¥	杯卖酒价格：	HKD55-480
¥	开瓶费：	HKD300
	酒单撰写人：	Mr. Akihiko Nosaka
	电　话：	852 37462733
	营业时间：	12：00-14：30，18：00-22：30（周一休）
	地　址：	香港九龙红磡环海街 11 号海名轩 5 楼
@	网　址：	www.kodining.com

莫尔顿牛排坊提供由美国谷物饲养而成的牛的牛肉、新鲜鱼类、波士顿大龙虾、羊排、鸡肉等美食。餐厅提供份大量足的牛排，包括上、T骨牛排 (1300 克)、顶级纽约西冷牛排 (550 克) 和双份特厚牛柳 (340 克)。

莫尔顿牛排坊还以丰富多样、备受好评的酒单而闻名遐迩。酒吧汇聚各种美酒佳酿，为客人提供各款顶级烈酒、各种国产和进口啤酒，还可调配各款极富创意的鸡尾酒，包括莫尔顿著名的"MORtinis"鸡尾酒。

MORTON'S THE STEAKHOUSE HONG KONG
莫尔顿牛排坊 – 香港

美式

酒单大奖专家评审团之酒单点评：

以红葡萄酒为主的酒单和以牛排为主的莫尔顿菜单交相辉映，为你带来顶级味觉享受。杯卖酒同样值得尝试，但横跨众多国家的国际酒单更耐人寻味，其中还有来自黎巴嫩的葡萄酒。一起来大口吃肉、大口喝酒吧！

An attractive list for Morton's steak-orientated menu with a red list that offers great depth for the carnivore attractions of the plate. By the glass is light-on, but a breadth of international wines goes a long way for interest, including a neat selection from Lebanon. Dig in.

¥	人均消费	HKD900-1200
¥	葡萄酒价格	$ $
	酒单酒款数	278
�!	杯卖酒款数	15
¥	杯卖酒价格	HKD110-380
¥	开瓶费	HKD400
	酒单撰写人	Miss Sylvia Lau
	电　话	852 27322343
	营业时间	17：30 - 23：00 (周一至周六)
		17：00 - 22：00 (周日)
	地　　址	香港九龙尖沙咀弥敦道 20 号
		喜来登酒店 4 楼
@	网　址	www.mortons.com

富丽堂皇的蚝酒吧是品尝香港最上乘海鲜的理想去处。 宾客们可在此一边享受美味的海鲜与葡萄酒，一边欣赏维多利亚港和香港天际线的壮丽景观。悉心周到的侍酒师会推荐与菜肴最相配的佳酿。牡蛎专家将对空运而至的新鲜牡蛎去壳进行检查，以供海鲜爱好者享用。从当季的优质水域采集到的约 25-30 种牡蛎，每日将以独特的口味和质感供客人品尝。

OYSTER & WINE BAR
蚝酒吧

欧陆式

酒单大奖专家评审团之酒单点评：

在国际上享誉盛名的酒款与多样的生蚝、国际范的菜单相得益彰。香槟是其一大特色，其次就是超过 50 款的杯卖酒包括了起泡酒、餐酒和甜酒。每款酒都配有相应的介绍，大大降低了选错酒的风险。

Plenty of internationally recognised drops to suit the extensive oyster selection or the globally influenced menu. Champagne's a specialty and there's over 50 sparkling, table and dessert wines by-the-glass. Helpful descriptions on each wine takes the guesswork out of choosing an unfamiliar label.

¥	人均消费	HKD1000
¥	葡萄酒价格	$ $ $
🍷	杯卖酒数	54
¥	杯卖酒价格	HKD95-480
¥	开 瓶 费	HKD500
👤	酒单撰写人	Mr. Roger Fan
📞	电　话	852 23691111
🕐	营业时间	18：30 - 23：00
		12：00 - 15：00（周日早午餐）
🏠	地　址	香港尖沙咀弥敦道 20 号
		喜来登酒店 18 楼
@	网　址	www.sheraton.com/hongkong

Room One 怡人的室内设计、特色饮品及酒吧小食和谐地融入酒店大堂。魅力灯光及动感节拍是香港人一天繁忙工作过后，放松心情、聚首畅饮的不二之选。Room One 呈献多款经典著名鸡尾酒以及来自世界各地的葡萄酒。口感微辛的 Concubine 鸡尾酒由新鲜薄荷、热情果伏特加、菠萝汁、自制辣椒糖浆调制而成。此外，酒吧更供应以干邑及茉莉糖浆调制而成的 eToasted Pineapple Martini 及创意 Perlini 汽泡特饮。

ROOM ONE

酒单大奖专家评审团之酒单点评：

作为 Room One 的姊妹酒单，这里只有一点不同。这是一个葡萄酒吧，但也有许多可供选择的鸡尾酒和开胃酒。威士忌的部分非常不错。他们还提供非常值得考虑的苏格兰和日本威士忌套餐。

The sister wine list to Room One with one major exception. This is a wine bar and there's plenty of pre-dinner action in the cocktail and aperitif list. The section on Whisky is outstanding. There's also the offer of a Scotch Flight and a Japanese whiskey flight, that is one well worth considering.

酒吧

¥	人均消费	HKD200
¥	葡萄酒价格	$ $
	酒单酒款数	32
	杯卖酒数	11
¥	杯卖酒价格	HKD95-175
¥	开瓶费	HKD350
	酒单撰写人	Mr. James Tamang
	电　话	852 23155888
	营业时间	15：00 - 01：00
	地　　址	香港九龙尖沙咀弥敦道 118 号 The Mira Hong Kong 地面大堂
@	网　址	www.themirahotel.com

St Betty——时尚休闲的现代欧式餐厅俯瞰维多利亚港。St Betty 是 Alan Yau 在香港开设的第一家餐厅，并由获得了两颗米其林星的著名伦敦厨师 Shane Osborn 领导。Shane 将法国技术与自身的澳大利亚背景相融合，打造一个现代欧洲菜单。St Betty 的设计理念是基于后现代意大利乡村厨房美学"Cucina Rustica"，以代表托斯卡纳和普罗旺斯的现代复兴精神。Andre Fu 的介入把"意大利乡村厨房"概想重新诠释，线条整洁，更加克制小节，设计具有功能性而不只是装饰。

ST BETTY RESTAURANT

现代欧式

酒单大奖专家评审团之酒单点评：

在找高性价比的酒款吗？不要寻别处，St Betty 就有。酒单虽短，酒款诱人且价格合理，尤其是无年份香槟和新世界酒款。杯卖酒风格各异且来源国家众多。美酒爱好者值得前往。

Looking for good value for money wines? Look no further. St Betty offers a small but enticing selection of wines at keen prices, notably non vintage Champagne and New World producers. Wines by the glass is an impressive cross-cut of styles and countries. Many wine lovers need go no further.

¥	人均消费：	HKD350
¥	葡萄酒价格：	$ $
♟	酒单酒款数：	132
🍷	杯卖酒款数：	19
¥	杯卖酒价格：	HKD45-140
¥	开瓶费：	HKD300
🙎	酒单撰写人：	Mr. Antonio Roveda
☎	电　话：	852 29792100
🕐	营业时间：	11：30 - 22：00（周一至周五）
		10，00 - 22，00（周末及公众假期）
🏠	地　址：	香港中环金融街 8 号 IFC 商场 2 楼 2075 号
@	网　址：	www.stbetty.com

Tapas Bar 洋溢现代气息且环境舒适，室内的宾客固然可尽览维多利亚港美景及城市景致，在户外雅座的宾客亦可从玻璃幕墙将美景尽收眼帘。Tapas Bar 供应来自超过 12 个国家的新旧世界美酒，当中包括论杯计算的红白美酒各 30 款，宾客亦可选享一系列香槟、鸡尾酒及无酒精鸡尾酒。Tapas Bar 内设有开放式厨房，呈献国际 tapas 小吃。

TAPAS BAR

  最佳杯卖酒酒单

酒单大奖专家评审团之酒单点评：

这是一份兼收英国、土耳其、希腊、保加利亚和一级庄的知名酒款的酒单。高性价比酒款不难找，试试意大利白或者罗讷河谷红吧。如果你还想找到特别一点的酒，那么这里还有价值港币 12500 的 1989 年 Domaine Leroy Corton。

An eclectic wine list where the wines of England, Turkey, Greece and Bulgaria mingle with First Growths and icons. Good value can be found here, look to the Italians whites and Rhone Valley reds, but should you call for something special keep in mind the Domaine Leroy Corton '89 for HK$12,500.

国际

¥	人均消费：	HKD300
¥	葡萄酒价格：	$ $
ₒ	酒单酒款数：	70
♈	杯卖酒数：	70
¥	杯卖酒价格：	HKD78-198
¥	开瓶费：	HKD385
☺	酒单撰写人：	Miss Yuen Yee Lam
☎	电　话：	852 27338775
⏱	营业时间：	15：30 - 01：00（周一至周五）
		12：00 - 01：00（周末及公众假期）
🏠	地　　址：	香港尖沙咀么地道 64 号九龙香格里拉大酒店地下大堂
@	网　　址：	www.shangri-la.com

The Press Room 于 2006 年开业，因原址位于 1920 年代乃华侨日报办事处，故餐厅得此名。The Press Room 每日提供午餐、晚餐；并于星期六、日提供周末早午餐。餐厅海鲜吧提供世界各地的精选新鲜生蚝及贝类，并且酒窖贮存了多款来自法国的葡萄美酒。特色菜式包括法式黑青口、香煎龙舌头柳伴牛油酱汁、精选烧烤及鲜果巧克力慕斯。

THE PRESS ROOM
（停业）

法式、欧式

酒单大奖专家评审团之酒单点评：

短小却不平庸的酒单与 The Press Room 设定的〝法国小酒馆〞主题相匹配。酒单另外展示了少见的卢瓦河谷、西南、朗格多克和汝哈酒，当然法国更有名的产区和有趣的酒款也榜上有名。价格也非常合理。

A smart, exciting small wine list totally in sync with the French bistro theme at The Press Room. Gives life to wines from the Loire, the South-West, Languedoc and the Jura as well as the more celebrated regions of France, and looks to some of the more exciting wine names of today. Prices are fair.

¥	人均消费	HKD160-500
¥	葡萄酒价格	＄ ＄
🍶	酒单酒款数	123
🍷	杯卖酒数	17
¥	杯卖酒价格	HKD58-104
¥	开瓶费	HKD290
👤	酒单撰写人	Mr. Max Poon
☎	电　话	852 25253444
⏰	营业时间	12：00 - 00：00（周一至周五）
		10：00 - 00：00（周末）
🏠	地　址	香港上环荷李活道 108 号
@	网　址	www.thepressroom.com.hk

The Principal 坐落于文化、创意和艺术色彩丰富的湾仔星街小区中心地段。由主厨 Jonay Armas 掌舵，主打新派欧陆菜式，餐单内容以优质食材主导，配合创新味道及技术，不断研发出惊喜十足的菜式。Jonay Armas 擅于以现代烹调手法演绎经典欧陆菜式，专注于食材本身的特质及精华，其菜式中亦可见日本及其他菜式的烹调元素，其独具创意的烹调风格及食材创新配搭，为客人带来耳目一新的美食体验。自 2011 年开业以来，餐厅已荣获《米其林指南 香港 澳门》2013 及 2014 年度米其林一星殊荣。

THE PRINCIPAL

  中国酒单大奖 – 决赛入围名单

现代欧式

酒单大奖专家评审团之酒单点评：

多么令人兴奋又充满现代风格的酒单！为那些量小但有趣的法国酒和其他酒点个赞。那些大胆又富有想象力的杯卖酒款更是让人无法自拔。别留恋于其中，继续看下去，你才不会错过更多出人意料的惊喜。

What an exciting and contemporary wine listing! Full marks for seeking out some of the smaller, more interesting producers in France and beyond. Bold and imaginative, the choices for Wines By The Glass are spot on making it hard to move on. But do move on! The back section is full of nice surprises.

¥	人均消费	HKD1,080
¥	葡萄酒价格	$ $
♙	杯卖酒数	21
¥	杯卖酒价格	HKD55-180
👥	酒单撰写人	Mr. Senki Ma
☎	电　话	852 25633444
⏰	营业时间	12：00 - 14：50,19：00 - 00：00（周一至周五）；19：00 - 00：00（周六）；12：00 - 17：30（周日）
🏠	地　址	香港湾仔星街 9 号
@	网　址	www.theprincipal.com.hk

Tosca 意大利餐厅的名字源自一部世界闻名的歌剧。餐厅楼底极高、设计独特，更备有开放式厨房。自 2013 年 4 月星级名厨 Pino Lavarra 掌舵后，Tosca 在短短八个月的时间内得到米芝莲一星评级，实在难得。大厨为宾客精心设计菜谱及烹调意大利南部特色美食，贯彻丽思卡尔顿酒店体贴入微的服务态度。

TOSCA

意式

酒单大奖专家评审团之酒单点评：

干得漂亮！Tosca 会让意大利酒爱好者为其酒单的广度与深度喝彩。热情的侍酒师 Ali Fong 将霞多丽赤霞珠与本土品种放在一起比拼。半瓶装和大瓶装也是特色。这是一匹黑马。

Bella! Tosca will make an Italian wine lover's heart sing such is its depth and breadth. The country is covered with enthusiasm by sommelier Ali Fong, who plays indigenous varieties off new stars like chardonnay or cabernet sauvignon. Half bottles and large formats abound. Mark ups are generous.

人均消费	HKD400-800
葡萄酒价格	$ $ $
酒单酒款数	890
杯卖酒数	24
杯卖酒价格	HKD120-580
开瓶费	HKD500
酒单撰写人	Mr. Ali Fong
电　话	852 22632270
营业时间	12：00-14：30，18：00-22：30
地　址	香港九龙柯士甸道西 1 号环球贸易广场丽思卡尔顿酒店 102 楼
网　址	www.ritzcarlton.com/en/Properties

来自意大利不同地区及传统历史留下的食谱带给大家地道的意大利美食。菜肴均为家庭传统烹调，如自制蛋面条、传统手做土豆团、坚持选用百分百初榨的意大利有机橄榄油来烹调食物、从意大利购入最高品质的食材。餐厅提供 20 个座位，给予大家一个轻松舒适、不花巧的氛围，就如置身于意大利家庭里享用居家菜肴一般。餐厅主人与来宾分享美酒及食物经验。葡萄酒、啤酒，汽水以及餐后酒均为意大利独有产品。葡萄酒单包含了意大利 20 种不同省份出产的葡萄酒，餐厅着意与大家分享当地独有的原产葡萄酒。

TRATTORIA CAFFE' MONTEVERDI
万特威尔意大利家庭小餐厅

酒单大奖专家评审团之酒单点评：

这是一份与餐厅的家常菜风格和谐共处、只关注意大利酒的酒单。小型的家族酒庄、本土葡萄品种是酒单的亮点，甚至某些濒临灭绝的本土品种也出现在酒单上。如果现存慢食酒单的话，那么非它莫属。非常好的价格，许多心头好。

A brilliant Italian-only wine listing in perfect harmony with Monteverdi's home style cooking. Small, family-run wineries are in the spotlight with indigenous grapes, sometimes close to extinction, featured prominently. A kind of Slow Food wine list if ever there was one. Great prices, lots of love.

意式

¥	人均消费	HKD150-500
¥	葡萄酒价格	$ $
▮▮	酒单酒款数	110
▮	杯卖酒款数	12
¥	杯卖酒价格	HKD68-78
¥	开瓶费	HKD350
☖	酒单撰写人	Mr. Armando Osmani
☎	电　话	852 25590115
◷	营业时间	12：00 - 15：00. 18：00 - 22：00（周一休）
⌂	地　　址	香港西营盘高街 6A
@	网　　址	www.monteverdi.com.hk

时尚、节拍、玩味尽在露天醉人酒廊 Vibes。位于 5 楼的 Vibes 为生活在快节奏的当代宾客呈献耳目一新的体验，在热情及充满动感的夜空下享用型格水烟、醉人鸡尾酒及经典小食，与城中最潮一族玩尽不夜天。

VIBES

酒单大奖专家评审团之酒单点评：

Vibes 是 Mira 里的一家会所。酒单虽短，然平易近人的酒款却非常多，开胃酒的部分更为其增色。招牌酒款和明星酒款也不在少数。美味的香槟鸡尾酒听上去是适合派对的佳酿。

Vibes is a lounge within The Mira complex boasting a small but highly accessible wine list coupled to an aperitif section devoted to, amongst others, Signature Liquids and Celebrations Shots. V-licious Champagne cocktail sounds particularly party hearty.

酒吧

人均消费	HKD230-250
葡萄酒价格：	$ $
酒单酒款数：	42
杯卖酒数：	10
杯卖酒价格：	HKD95-175
开 瓶 费：	HKD350
酒单撰写人：	Mr. Austin Moreno
电 话：	852 23155999
营业时间：	17：00 - 01：00
地 址：	香港九龙尖沙咀弥敦道 118 号 The Mira Hong Kong 5 楼
网 址：	www.themirahotel.com

Whisk 格调时尚典雅且舒适，展示最优秀之厨艺及最顶尖的精致当代欧陆美馔。餐厅格调时尚典雅，其贵宾厅及华丽的"主厨餐桌"为客人带来味觉及视觉上的极致享受。大厨精心挑选时令食材入馔，配以多款价格相宜的醇厚佳酿，为饕客带来难忘的餐饮体验。餐厅备有单点菜谱、品味菜谱和快捷午餐。

WHISK

酒单大奖专家评审团之酒单点评：

这份酒单更像是以价格为核心而创建，或者说以"价格至上"的经营理念。合理的价格会让许多食客尝试到顶级酒款，比如 Vega Sicilia、吉加乐和品牌香槟。不管怎样，这些欧洲酒款的价格都很合理。

This is a wine list built around price or, rather as the management promotes "extremely attractive prices." They are, indeed, very keen, which will allow many a diner to go upmarket, maybe to Vega Sicilia, Guigal or grand marque Champagne - all very affordable from this strong cast of Europeans.

欧式

¥	人均消费：	HKD250-1000
¥	葡萄酒价格：	$ $
	酒单酒款数：	208
	杯卖酒数：	14
¥	杯卖酒价格：	HKD45-130
¥	开 瓶 费：	HKD350
	酒单撰写人：	Mr. William Fu
	电 话：	852 23155999
	营业时间：	12：00 - 14：30, 18：30 - 23：00（周二至周六）；12：00 - 15：00（周日）
	地 址：	香港九龙尖沙咀弥敦道 118 号 The Mira Hong Kong 5 楼
@	网 址：	www.themirahotel.com

Yamm 拥有偌大面积，餐厅室内设计创新别致，并配有瞩目的灯光效果及柔和音乐，营造私密舒适的环境。餐厅屡获殊荣，呈献令人垂涎的美食、餐饮、果汁及特色茗茶，缔造无可比拟的自助餐体验。

YAMM

国际

酒单大奖专家评审团之酒单点评：

朴实但不简单的酒单适合 Mira 酒店——这个以汉堡包和意面为主角的餐厅。实惠的价格和 Two Paddocks 黑皮诺的奇异酒款定能满足爱好者的需求。以葡萄酒风格作分类让选酒之路顺畅不少。

A simple but attractive wine list suited to the burger-pasta informality of The Mira. Prices are keen and the odd little find like Two Paddocks pinot noir will surely make a wine lover's day. Wine listed by style helps the wine search go smoothly.

🍷	人均消费	HK$288-668
¥	葡萄酒价格	$ $
🍾	酒单酒款数	35
🍷	杯卖酒数	11
¥	杯卖酒价格	HKD95-105
¥	开 瓶 费	HKD350
👥	酒单撰写人	Mr. Alan Sun
☎	电　　话	852 23681111
🕐	营业时间	06：00 - 00：00
🏠	地　　址	香港九龙尖沙咀弥敦道 118 号
		The Mira Hong Kong 大堂
@	网　　址	www.themirahotel.com

玉蕾为食客呈献正宗上海佳肴——大厨以无限创意将传统菜式化为艺术品，招牌菜包括九州醉蟹及生炒鲍片。餐厅的午市亦供应广东点心及烧味。玉蕾以"中式花卉"为设计概念，5间贵宾房分别以花朵命名，每间房的水晶灯及壁画皆切合相应的主题花卉。在奖项方面，餐厅获得《米其林指南 香港 澳门》颁发 2013 及 2014 年度一星荣誉，其他奖项包括"*Hong Kong Tatler*"杂志之 2013 及 2014 年度"香港及澳门最佳食府"、《南华早报》之"100 Top Tables 2014"。

YU LEI
玉蕾

  最佳香槟酒单 – 香港、澳门及台湾地区

酒单大奖专家评审团之酒单点评：

这里有许多只有胆大的食客才能享有的美食：猪胃、鸡肾和猪肠。这些与中国烈酒或日本清酒极搭。此外，这份酒单也不乏世界各大顶级酒款。

There are some mighty adventurous food tastes here: pig's stomach, chicken kidney and pork intestine that may see diners heading for the Chinese spirits or Japanese sake listings (which are excellent). Otherwise, this exceptional list is up to the task with an exhaustive array of top world wines.

上海菜式

¥	人均消费	HKD500-2000
¥	葡萄酒价格	$ $ $
🍷	酒单酒款数	1903
♟	杯卖酒数	22
¥	杯卖酒价格	HKD55-480
¥	开瓶费	HKD300
👤	酒单撰写人	Mr. Akihiko Nosaka
☎	电　话	852 37462788
⏱	营业时间	12：00-14：30，18：00-22：30（周一休）
🏠	地　　址	香港九龙红磡环海街 11 号海名轩 5 楼
@	网　址	www.kodining.com

MARQUIS DE
MONTESQUIOU
RARE ARMAGNAC

蒙特伯爵

雅文邑 白兰地

稀有年份系列

Millésime

乐享美酒需理性

智利－美酒天堂

多样化的气候 · 纯净的土地
没有污染 · 无需嫁接
完美的葡萄产区 · 带来名庄佳酿

VIÑA VENTISQUERO
A step beyond

Vina Ventisquero（西班牙语译为冰川酒庄）在1998年成立，该酒庄的背景是智利最大的食品集团Agrosuper。酒庄位于Maipo Valley迈朴山谷海岸山脉地区，是由一群富有开创性、企业家精神的年轻队伍管理着，最重要的是他们对葡萄酒充满激情短短十几年间便迅速崛起，一跃成为智利排名前十的酒庄之一。冰川葡萄酒也是新世界中唯一一个在米其林全球50家餐厅排名第一至第五中都可以品尝到的，我非常自豪！

中国总代理：杭州唐源贸易有限公司　网址：www.tangyuanwine.com　联系电话：0571-88303381

此GRANDES VINOS高端系列出自于智利VSPT集团。VSPT是智利第二大的葡萄酒出口商，已进驻中国10年多，是国内最著名的智利葡萄酒酿造厂商之一，有着悠久的历史和传承。VSPT旗下酒庄在智利的有Sanpedro, Tarapaca, Santa Helena, Misiones de Rengo,Altair, Vi-na Mar, Casa Rivas和Vina Leyda。每个酒庄都拥有属于它们自己的独一无二的品牌和此产区最具代表地域性的优质葡萄酒。

中国办事处：上海市闵行区金汇路463弄28号B栋4楼A座
网址：www.vsptwines.com 联系电话：021-61517879 邮箱：VSPTCHINA@163.COM

COLECCIÓN
DEL PRESIDENTE

安帝雅酒庄由智利著名酿酒师Alvaro Espinoza创立，是智利第一个车库酒酒庄，也是一个有机和生物动力学酒庄。Antiyal被《葡萄酒观察家》（《Wine Spe-ctator》）誉为是一款"Chile Returns to Its Roots"的酒，被《葡萄酒爱好者》评为12款必须尝试的智利酒之一。

总统收藏系列葡萄酒是智利葡萄酒领导品牌De Mar-tino酒庄为了纪念中智两国自由关税贸易协定在酒庄里签订这一伟大时刻而创立的具有历史意义的品牌。该系列葡萄酒酿自智利优秀产区，同一位置同样起源的葡萄园，表达出葡萄酒独一无二的起源意义和风土特点。

中智美景
进口商：中智美景贸易有限公司
网址：www.zzmeijing.com 联系电话：021-55135628 邮箱：zzmeijing01@163.com

RIOJA-the best food pairing wine on earth!

里奥哈 - 地球上最佳配餐葡萄酒

里奥哈优质原产地(D.O.Ca Rioja)

优质葡萄酒的保证

葡萄酒产业中的D.O.（原产地)是指一个葡萄酒的产区，
这个产区的酒庄都必须按照特定的质量管控标准来进行
酿制。这个概念类似于法国的AOC (Apellations
d'Origine Controlée)。所以，在选购D.O.标志的葡萄酒
时，消费者可以确信这款酒从葡萄种植、葡萄收获到最
终酿制的全过程都是在严格的质量控制下进行的。另外
，葡萄酒的装瓶过程也必须在产地内完成。

里奥哈产区早在1926年就成为了西班牙第一个获得原
产地的地区，同时也是西班牙最负盛名的葡萄酒产区。
在1991年，里奥哈产区更是因为其贯穿酿造全过程的
精益求精的质量标准而进一步获得了优质原产地
(D.O.Ca)，也就是认证产区的业内最高资格。

里奥哈产区管理委员会投入大量精力以确保里奥哈优质
原产地产区只出品质量上乘的顶级美酒。

所以消费者只需认准里奥哈优质原产地的标志，就可以

放心选购到高品质的葡萄酒！

GUARANTEE OF FINE WINE

A Designation of Origin (D.O.) for Wine is a
wine-producing region whose wineries are subject to
specific quality control rules, it is similar to the French
Apellations d'Origine Controlée (AOC). Therefore,
when you choose a D.O. wine you can be sure strict
quality controls have been followed all through the
viticulture, harvest and winemaking. Also, the wines
must be bottled within the production area.

D.O. Rioja, as the most relevant wine region in Spain,

was the first one awarded the title D.O., in 1926. Then,
in 1991 D.O. Rioja was awarded the highest category
– Qualified D.O., or D.O.Ca. - because of its even
stricter quality controls all through the process,
making Rioja the first D.O. in Spain to be so honoured.

The Rioja Control Board works hard to ensure D.O.Ca.

Rioja offers the world only the best, premium, Fine
Wines.

Remember, if you want Fine Wines, the D.O.Ca.
Rioja seal is the best guarantee !

 里奥哈官方微博
(Rioja Weibo):
里奥哈优质原产地
中国推广机构

RIOJa
西班牙里奥哈
葡萄酒优质原产地

奥罗拉坐拥澳门半岛醉人美景。主厨 Michele dell' Aquila 通过意大利南部普利亚省的烹调方法，带宾客进入引人入胜的南意美馔世界。菜式以各式鲜鱼及海产为主，并融入地中海风味。奥罗拉设有户外露台，并坐拥壮丽海景，让客人们开怀品尝美食。

AURORA
奥罗拉

意式

酒单大奖专家评审团之酒单点评：

这份几近完美的酒单内含优质和有代表性的酒款。让人口水直流！60 个年份的拉图（1945—2005）是多么爆炸性的开篇，随之而来的便都是法国、意大利和其他国家的名庄。酒友有福了。半瓶装和大瓶装也很丰富。

A near faultless wine list that pulses with quality and iconic wine names. Highly mouthwatering! It starts with a Bang! with a vertical of Latour (1945-2005) and what follows is a game of tag between France and Italy and the rest of the world. The drinker wins. Half bottles and magnums aplenty too.

¥	人均消费：	MOP600
¥	葡萄酒价格：	$ $ $
♨	酒单酒款数：	650
♀	杯卖酒数：	18
¥	杯卖酒价格：	MOP80-160
¥	开 瓶 费：	MOP400
☺	酒单撰写人：	Mr. Keith Lam
☏	电　话：	853 28868868
⏰	营业时间：	11：30-14：30（周一至周六）
		11：30-15：30（周日）;18：00-22：30
🏠	地　址：	澳门氹仔广东大马路新濠锋 10 楼
@	网　址：	www.altiramacau.com

灵感源自 20 世纪 30 年代法国雅韵，宝雅座为宾客呈上精湛绝伦的法式美食艺术。在慵懒午后，宾客步入宝雅座露台，沐浴温暖阳光，小小品味优雅法式下午茶，或是在晚餐时刻惬意安坐，享用一餐丰盛的法式佳肴，品尝总厨 Elie Khalife 特别为宾客奉上的顶级巴来风味甜点。

Mr. Adolphus Foo

AUX BEAUX ARTS RESTAURANT
宝雅座

法式

酒单大奖专家评审团之酒单点评：

此单只因天上有！经过六年酝酿而成的酒单包罗万象，出色的、有代表性的、纯正的，甚至是奇葩的酒款应有尽有。有人听说过日本起泡酒吗？最后还有 Palace Bacaco、Famille Becot 和 Luis Pato 在等着诱惑你。

A magnum opus! A wine list six years in the making that reflects the beautiful, the iconic, the solid gold performers and the strangely eclectic. A Japanese sparkling wine anyone? If one should reach the end, the temptation of wine alliances with Palace Bacaco, Famille Becot and Luis Pato await.

¥	人均消费	MOP680
¥	葡萄酒价格	$ $ $
🍷	酒单酒款数	1450
🍷	杯卖酒数	14
¥	杯卖酒价格	MOP45-220
¥	开瓶费	MOP300
👤	酒单撰写人	Mr. Adolphus Foo
📞	电 话	853 88028888
🕐	营业时间	11：00 - 15：00（周末早午餐）
		18：00 - 00：00（周二至周日）
🏠	地 址	澳门外港新填海区孙逸仙大马路
@	网 址	www.mgmmacau.com

贝隆是澳门悦榕庄之特色食府之一，以法国布列塔尼沿海地区的名产——贝隆蚝命名。餐厅位于31楼，壮丽无比的路氹环回美景尽收眼帘。贝隆以海洋世界为设计主调，宾客刚入餐厅，便感觉犹如潜入深海一般，享受豪华体验。贝隆提供时尚创新的经典欧陆烧烤菜式及顶级海鲜珍馐，而且厨师会在餐桌旁精心烹制部分特色菜肴，缔造互动美食体验。而别具一格的酒窖收藏了一系列澳门罕有的独特珍品，这些都出产于法国、葡萄牙、意大利、南非、澳大利亚、新西兰以及美国的顶尖酒厂。

BELON
贝隆

欧式

酒单大奖专家评审团之酒单点评：

不论是龙利鱼、挪威鲭、科罗拉多羊排，还是智利黑鲈，这里的酒单和菜单一样地包罗万象。哪怕是泰国希拉也榜上有名。响亮的品牌自然要价不菲，但性价比高的酒款和绝佳的起泡酒也触手可及。

Just as you can order Dover sole, Norwegian mackerel, Colorado lamb and Chilean sea bass off the food menu here, expect a similarly expansive world wine list. Even a Thai syrah gets a listing! Big names abound, at big prices, but there are also some star finds along with an excellent fizz component.

¥	人均消费：	MOP950
¥	葡萄酒价格：	$ $ $
♟	酒单酒款数：	197
♟	杯卖酒数：	11
¥	杯卖酒价格：	MOP90-218
¥	开瓶费：	MOP300
♙	酒单撰写人：	Mr. Andy Tam
☏	电　话：	853 88838833
⏱	营业时间：	18：00 - 23：00（周二休）
⌂	地　址：	澳门路氹城莲花海滨大马路银河悦榕庄 31 楼
@	网　址：	www.banyantree.com/zh/cn-china-macau

在主厨麦伟明师傅带领下，喜粤不仅供应美味粤式料理，更精心炮制中国各地风味的健康餐点。餐厅以中国红为主要色调，以圆弧形排列的垂帘为餐厅增添现代感。喜粤被列入《米其林指南 香港 澳门 2013》"上佳的餐厅"，亦被"*Hong Kong Tatler*"杂志选为"2014 年最佳餐厅之一"。

CANTON RESTAURANT
喜粤

粤式

酒单大奖专家评审团之酒单点评：

你的那杯酒是什么？这里有来自波尔多一级庄，意大利巴罗洛以及一些经济型的澳洲和西班牙的红白酒。开一瓶价值澳币 9990 或葡币 72000 的 82 年拉菲怎么样？喜欢奇珍异宝的你也能有所收获。

What's your drink? There are plenty of options here from Bordeaux First Growths and Italian Barolos through to some economical Aussie and Spanish reds and whites. Special occasion wines are a specialty. How about a '82 Lafite for AU$9990 or MOP72,000? The odd gem can also be found.

¥	人均消费	MOP400
¥	葡萄酒价格	$ $ $
⌁	酒单酒款数	592
♟	杯卖酒数	8
¥	杯卖酒价格	MOP40-210
¥	开瓶费	MOP400
☻	酒单撰写人	Mr. Jimmy Valentine
☏	电　话	853 81189930
⌚	营业时间	11：00 - 15：00，18：00 - 23：00
⌂	地　址	澳门凼仔路凼金光大道望德圣母湾大马路澳门威尼斯人度假村酒店赌场层 1018 铺
@	网　址	www.venetianmacao.com

　"当奥丰素 1890 意式料理"于 2007 年在澳门新葡京酒店开业，由享誉国际的厨师 Alfonso Iaccarino 主理。Iaccarino 先生的家族数代以烹调技艺卓越而闻名，他们所经营的餐厅在意大利南部荣获米其林二星级荣誉。"当奥丰素 1890 意式料理"把简单而上乘的材料，创制出最正宗的意大利南部传统高级菜式。
　"当奥丰素 1890 意式料理"除了提供令人难忘的精致美食，还提供超过 14000 款各国名酒佳酿，与综合城的其余 13 间餐厅共用。

DON ALFONSO 1890
当奥丰素 1890 意式料理

意大利南部式

酒单大奖专家评审团之酒单点评：

这是另一张以新葡京酒店库藏巨大的酒窖为基础而设计的酒单。为了与餐点相搭，直接找瓶意大利红葡萄酒、皮埃蒙特或托斯卡纳佳酿来佐餐吧。相较之下，意大利白葡萄酒则少得多（尽管酒单上有数不清的勃艮第白葡萄酒）。

Another list drawing from the vast cellar of the Grand Hotel Lisboa. In keeping with the cuisine, skip to the Italian reds and choose from pages of Piedmontese and Tuscan glories. The Italian white selection is comparatively small (though the tempting list of white Burgundy is seemingly endless!).

¥	人均消费	MOP300-1590
¥	葡萄酒价格	$ $ $
♟	酒单酒款数	14000
♟	杯卖酒款数	9
¥	杯卖酒价格	MOP130-200
¥	开瓶费	MOP400
♟	酒单撰写人	Mr. Paul Lo
☎	电　话	853 88037722
◷	营业时间	12：00-14：30，18：30-22：30
⌂	地　址	澳门葡京路新葡京酒店 3 楼
@	网　址	www.grandlisboahotel.com

Mr. Arnaud Echalier

"朝"特设八个以中国八大朝代命名的私人包厢，每个包厢均以中式庙檐相隔，采用历朝特有的装潢设计。大厅风格经典，采用对称格局设计，大红灯笼高挂于天花的雕花木横梁上。瓷器设计精致，与公用及私人筷子相映成趣，而银器餐具镌刻着巴来名品"Ercuis"标志。酒窖贮藏着400多种陈年佳酿。茶茗则会根据天然茶色挑选并搭配非透明或半透明的精致茶壶。"朝"的美味佳肴包括弹牙爽口的开胃海蜇小食配以清甜的腌制小红茄、每天新鲜准备的限量鱼子酱大虾及五香炸蟹钳、入口即溶的川味干煸牛肉、即点即制时蔬、各色泽果拼盘以及以奶黄为馅料的香脆芝麻丸子，其口感软熟香甜，无不令人垂涎欲滴。

DYNASTY 8
朝

中式

酒单大奖专家评审团之酒单点评：

充斥着波尔多和赤霞珠的这份酒单很对中国酒友的胃口。大部分的波尔多名庄都尽显其中。然而，一旦跳出法国部分，你就会有更多选择。在知名酒商的二级酒款中，你总会挑选到性价比高的一款。

A wine list that plays to the Chinese wine lover's interest in Bordeaux and cabernet sauvignon. Most of the big Bordeaux names are here. However, look outside France and there's plenty to enjoy. Good value can be found in second labels from known producers.

¥	人均消费：	MOP500
¥	葡萄酒价格：	$ $ $
♟	酒单酒款数：	501
♟	杯卖酒款数：	18
¥	杯卖酒价格：	HKD30-165
¥	开 瓶 费：	HKD400-600
🧑	酒单撰写人：	Mr. Arnaud Echalier
☎	电 话：	853 81138920
🕐	营业时间：	11：00-15：00，18：00-23：00（周日至周四）；18：00-00：00（周五至周六）
🏠	地 址：	澳门金沙城中心地面层
@	网 址：	conradhotels3.hilton.com/en/hotels/macao

置身于充满传统葡萄牙风味的氛围，沉醉于葡轩所带来的正宗葡式美馔及地道澳门菜，葡轩让客人们以味蕾重温澳葡历史。

GOSTO
葡轩

现代葡澳菜式

酒单大奖专家评审团之酒单点评：

"葡轩"选择了许多葡萄牙酒，但是"精选"中有更多的大品牌，从 Drouhin 到玛歌，Tenuta Dell'Ornellaia 到 Felton Road。也许真正的酒款隐藏在这些推荐酒之后。如果打算在这里找到合适的酒款，那么你就需要多花点儿时间。别忘了给波特酒留些余地。

Gosto pays homage to Portugal supported by a plethora of marquee wines under its various 'Collections' from Drouhin to Margaux, Tenuta Dell'Ornellaia to Felton Road. Possibly the real action follows these introductory lists. A tricky list to navigate, take your time. And leave room for the Ports!

人均消费：	MOP250
葡萄酒价格：	$ $ $
酒单酒款数：	762
杯卖酒数：	10
杯卖酒价格：	MOP52-98
开瓶费：	MOP300
酒单撰写人：	Mr. Eugene Tan
电　话：	853 88832221
营业时间：	12：00-15：00,18：00-23：00(周一至周五) 12：00-23：00(周末及公众假期)
地　址：	澳门"澳门银河"综合度假城地下 G21
网　址：	www.galaxyentertainment.com

葡国餐厅是葡萄牙著名其林星级餐厅 Fortaleza do Guincho 的首间海外分店，提供高级精致葡式料理。在装潢搭配上，餐厅采用了瑰丽温馨的颜色作主调，置身这优雅的环境中，客人可充分感受到浓厚葡国风情。葡国餐厅严选最上乘食材，融合其精湛创新的烹调方式，令传统葡式料理提升至另一境界。葡国餐厅在提供顶级佳肴的同时，还有超过 14000 款来自世界各地的名酒佳酿，与综合城的其余 13 间餐厅共用。

GUINCHO A GALERA
葡国餐厅

葡式

酒单大奖专家评审团之酒单点评：

尽管它厚如辞典，你也应该直奔葡萄牙酒的部分，让美食与美酒相聚。但前路漫漫，诱惑太多！罗列了 12780 款的酒单让人惊讶又欣喜。每个都是顶级酒款。记得给甜品（甜酒）留点地方就好。

Of course you should head straight to the Portuguese wines on this mega wine list to get the true synergy of food and wine happening but what temptations are strewn in your path! This extraordinary 12,780 wines listing will amaze and delight. Truly world class. Just leave room for dessert (wine).

¥	人均消费：	MOP280-1000
¥	葡萄酒价格：	$ $ $
🍷	酒单酒款数：	14000
🍷	杯卖酒数：	9
¥	杯卖酒价格：	MOP80-250
¥	开 瓶 费：	MOP400
👤	酒单撰写人：	Mr. Paul Lo
☎	电 话：	853 88037676
⏰	营业时间：	12：00 - 14：30，18：30 - 22：30
🏠	地 址：	澳门葡京路 2-4 号葡京酒店西座 3 楼
@	网 址：	www.hotelisboa.com

获得米其林星级荣誉的"誉珑轩"为宾客带来极致珍馐、精雕玉馔，缔造全城最尊尚的粤式餐飨体验。由名厨谭国锋带领的专业厨师团队，于新濠天地创新演绎世界各地鲜活食材及地道美馔，华丽装潢以及殷勤的贴心服务，让贵客体会更高层次的多元感官享受。

JADE DRAGON
誉珑轩

粤式

酒单大奖专家评审团之酒单点评：

这家的酒单与TTR有很多重合之处，但这次搭配的是粤菜。对于法国红葡萄酒爱好者而言，这简直就是阿拉丁山洞，诸多宝藏都让人爱不释手。还有木桐酒庄64个年份（1945-2009）任君挑选。当然，价位也跟酒款一样，水平很高。

Jade Dragon shares the same wines with The Tasting Room, but this time the food theme is Cantonese. An Aladdin's Cave for lovers of French reds and should the fancy take you, there's always the vertical of Mouton-Rothschild (1945-2009) to take home! Prices, as you might expect, are on the high side.

¥	人均消费：	MOP700-1200
¥	葡萄酒价格：	$ $ $
酒	酒单酒款数：	750
¥	杯卖酒款数：	7
¥	杯卖酒价格：	MOP70-218
¥	开瓶费：	MOP400
👤	酒单撰写人：	Mr. Mathieu Gaignon
📞	电　话：	853 88682822
🕐	营业时间：	11：00 - 15：00, 18：00 - 23：00
🏠	地　址：	澳门路氹连贯公路新濠天地新濠大道2楼
@	网　址：	www.cityofdreamsmacau.com.cn

莫尔顿牛排坊供应美国上等牛肉以及各类新鲜鱼类、龙虾、牛仔肉和鸡。餐厅的每个分店供应一致的菜式，牛扒份量特大，包括 24 安士上等腰肉牛扒、20 安士顶级纽约西冷扒和 14 安士双份特厚牛柳。各店备有各式酒类饮品和各种获奖的世界名酿。

MORTON'S MACAU
莫尔顿牛排坊 － 澳门

美式

酒单大奖专家评审团之酒单点评：

莫尔顿牛排坊连锁自然是专注于美国酒的餐厅。不要浪费机会，快来品尝卡内罗斯的霞多丽、威拉米特河谷的黑皮诺、纳帕的赤霞珠。也别忘了看看其余产区的酒款，欧洲红葡萄酒小分队也是不容小觑的。

The Morton's Chicago Steak House franchise concentrates on American wines, naturally, so dig in to those Carneros chardonnays, Willamette Valley pinot noirs and Napa cabernets but do leave room to explore the rest of this tight little listing. The European red wine contingent is especially strong.

¥	人均消费	MOP900-1000
¥	葡萄酒价格	$ $
	酒单酒款数	145
	杯卖酒数	15
¥	杯卖酒价格	MOP90-195
¥	开 瓶 费	MOP300
	酒单撰写人	Mr. Simon Graham
☎	电 话	853 81175000
⏰	营业时间	17：00 - 23：00
🏠	地 址	澳门氹仔路氹金光大道望得圣母湾大马路澳门威尼斯人度假村酒店大运河购物中心 1016 铺
@	网 址	www.mortons.com

　"北方馆"汇聚中国东北及四川美食精髓，精心炮制各式经典佳肴。"北方馆"内设有开放式厨房，让客人欣赏厨师即席制作及烹调手工拉面、水饺及各式蒸点。所有菜式均是由来自东北的厨师烹调而成最正宗的地方料理。

　被"*Hong Kong Tatler*"杂志选为"2014年最佳餐厅之一"的"北方馆"，由优美的传统木制间格及装饰布置而成，并以北方及四川美食佳肴见称。

NORTH RESTAURANT
北方馆

酒单大奖专家评审团之酒单点评：

热辣来袭！"北方馆"是中国东北偏辣菜系的一家餐厅，所以在选酒时，你需要格外地注意。这份有592款的超强酒单带你环游世界，流连于意大利、法国和美国。还有许多值得一掷千金的酒款。

The heat's on! The North is home to some fiery chilli-led North-East China cooking so take care in your wine selections. The 592-strong wine list offers an intriguing trip around the world, lingering on Italy, France and the US. There's plenty of splurge targets so enjoy.

东北菜式

¥	人均消费：	MOP300
¥	葡萄酒价格：	$ $ $
	酒单酒款数：	592
	杯卖酒数：	8
¥	杯卖酒价格：	MOP40-210
¥	开瓶费：	MOP400
	酒单撰写人：	Mr. Jimmy Valentine
	电　话：	853 81189980
	营业时间：	11：00 - 23：00（周四至周日）
		11：00 - 02：00 （周五及周六）
	地　　址：	澳门凼仔路凼金光大道望得圣母湾大马路澳门威尼斯人度假村酒店赌场层 1015 铺
@	网　　址：	www.venetianmacao.com

澳门威尼斯人满载意国滋味新体验。餐厅设计时尚，供应地道的经典意大利美食。另外还设有露天用餐区，让宾客将泳池碧波美景尽收眼底。无论做何选择，这里都能让人全情醉心于意大利氛围之中，满足而归！

"碧涛意国渔乡"被 *"Hong Kong Tatler"* 杂志评为"2014年最佳餐厅之一"。

PORTOFINO RESTAURANT
碧涛意国渔乡

意式

酒单大奖专家评审团之酒单点评：

作为澳门最佳葡萄酒场所之一，"碧涛意国渔乡"以优质的意大利饮食与极好的意大利酒单来维护其声誉。干得漂亮！巴罗洛的酒款尤为引人注目。波尔多和美国酒的爱好者也不会失望的。这里也有不少的中国烈酒可供选择。

Portofino cements its reputation as one of Macau's finest wine establishments with Italian inspired cooking matched by a stunning Italian wine list. Bravo! The Barolo selection is particularly exciting. Bordeaux and US wine lovers won't be disappointed. There's a good list of Chinese spirits too.

¥	人均消费	MOP380
¥	葡萄酒价格	$ $
	酒单酒款数	592
	杯卖酒数	16
¥	杯卖酒价格	MOP65-400
¥	开瓶费	MOP400
	酒单撰写人	Mr. Jimmy Valentine
	电话	853 81189950
	营业时间	11：00 - 15：00，18：00 - 23：00
	地址	澳门凼仔路凼金光大道望得圣母湾大马路澳门威尼斯人度假村酒店赌场层 1039 铺
@	网址	www.venetianmacao.com

被誉为是全亚洲最顶尖餐厅之一的天巢法国餐厅，自 2009 年到 2014 年间，成为全澳唯一连续六年获《米其林指南 香港 澳门》颁发三星荣誉的高级食府。餐厅拥有区内品种最齐全的美酒餐单，酒窖珍藏超过 14000 款来自世界各地的名酒佳酿。天巢法国餐厅由全球获得最多米其林星级荣誉的名厨 Joël Robuchon 先生亲自主理，为顾客提供传统高级的法式佳肴。

ROBUCHON AU DOME
天巢法国餐厅

  名人堂

法式

酒单大奖专家评审团之酒单点评：

这是一份由世界顶级又罕见的甜酒、红白勃艮第（按产区排序）以及波尔多汇集而成的酒单，多么地令人震惊！还有超过 80 页的半瓶装、40 页的大瓶装可选。新世界的名酒、经典的香槟和各种佳酿都可杯卖。与去年相比，酒单增加了新年份和拍卖得来的酒款。

A stunning collection of the world's greatest - and rarest - sweet wines, white & red Burgundy (arranged by appellation) and Bordeaux. 80+ pages of half bottles, 40+ of magnums. Big reds from the new world, classy Champagne, ultra-fine wines by glass. Updated with new releases/auction purchases.

¥	人均消费：	MOP498-2300
¥	葡萄酒价格：	$ $ $
🍷	酒单酒款数：	14000
🍷	杯卖酒数：	20
¥	杯卖酒价格：	MOP140-400
¥	开瓶费：	MOP400
👤	酒单撰写人：	Mr. Paul Lo
☎	电　话：	853 88037878
🕐	营业时间：	12：00-14：30,18：30-22：30
🏠	地　址：	澳门葡京路新葡京酒店 43 楼
@	网　址：	www.grandlisboahotel.com

Mr. Paul Lo

顶级天妇罗料理与澳门半岛环回美景融为一体，带来味觉与视觉的双重享受。"天政"主厨的一双巧手，不仅于常见菜式之中展现极致厨艺，更确保料理烹调得恰到好处，外皮脆而不腻，里面鲜嫩可口。"天政"配备传统榻榻米座位、精致的私人包厢，更特别设有寿司台和清酒廊，引领宾客探索传统日本美食文化。

TENMASA
天政

  澳门地区最佳葡萄酒酒单

酒单大奖专家评审团之酒单点评：

"天政"与"奥罗拉"餐厅的酒单都包含了详尽且优质的酒款，除了前六页的顶级清酒。这里有太多可供选择的酒款，因此你会需要一些时间来做决定。回头客的产生也是有原因的。

Tenmasa shares the same exhaustive, quality wine list as Aurora restaurant with one major exception: six pages of superlative sakes to start. There is simply so much choice to be found here, that making a decision could prove time consuming! A good enough reason for a return visit.

日式

¥	人均消费	MOP1000
¥	葡萄酒价格	$ $ $
🍷	酒单酒款数	650
🍷	杯卖酒数	18
¥	杯卖酒价格	MOP80-160
¥	开瓶费	MOP400
👤	酒单撰写人	Mr. Andrew Wong
☎	电　话	853 28868868
🕐	营业时间	12：00-14：30，18：00-22：30（周一休）
🏠	地　址	澳门氹仔广东大马路新濠锋 11 楼
@	网　址	www.altiramacau.com

庭园意大利餐厅满泻着意国的温情风韵，坚信"只有诚意和热枕，才能为宾客带来最佳的餐喝体验"。厨师们从优质的时令食材得到了灵感，并结合了新派的料理构思，创出一道道正宗的意国佳肴。

TERRAZZA
庭园意大利餐厅

意式

酒单大奖专家评审团之酒单点评：

在这里，只有想不到，没有点不到——不论是多佛鳎挪威鲭、科罗拉多羊排，还是智利黑鲈。酒单也是如此（泰国酒也名列其中）。大品牌的价格自然是不低的，但是性价比高的酒款也比比皆是。

Just as you can order Dover sole, Norwegian mackerel, Colorado lamb and Chilean sea bass here, expect to see a similarly expansive wine list devoted to world wine (and that includes Thailand). Big names, sometimes with big price tags, sit side by side with some truly interesting selections.

¥	人均消费：	MOP500
	葡萄酒价格：	$ $ $
	酒单酒款数：	762
	杯卖酒数：	18
	杯卖酒价格：	MOP67-248
	开瓶费：	MOP300
	酒撰写人：	Mr. Eugene Tan
	电　话：	853 88832221
	营业时间：	18：00 - 23：00（周日休）
	地　址：	澳门"银河酒店"2楼201
@	网　址：	www.galaxyentertainment.com

澳门唯一荣获《米其林指南 香港 澳门 2014》颁发三星荣誉的高级中菜食府 "8 餐厅" 主打精致广东料理。餐厅由香港著名设计师陈幼坚设计，他把寓意活力十足的金鱼和象征吉祥富贵的 "8" 字巧妙地融汇在其室内设计中，气派独特而又极富传统中国特色。餐厅提供的菜式种类数不胜数，中午推出的创意点心更多达 50 余款，让宾客尽情享受的优雅又富有创意的美食体验。"8 餐厅" 为深谙美食之道的宾客供应佳酿，均由葡京酒店集团综合城的酒窖提供。酒窖内收藏超过 14000 款各国名酒，与综合城内其余 13 间餐厅共用。

THE EIGHT
8 餐厅

粤式

酒单大奖专家评审团之酒单点评：

如此美味的粤菜绝对值得品味，恰似那豪华的酒单与装修风格一样。餐厅的酒窖跟新葡京酒店在一起。世界顶级产区的酒款任君挑选，没有喝不到，只有想不到。

Cantonese food this good deserves a wine list as lavish as the décor (complete with giant projected goldfish)! Thankfully the restaurant draws upon the vast cellar of the Grand Lisboa Hotel. Every wine wish comes true with mind-blowing selections from the world's greatest regions.

¥	人均消费：	MOP350-1,500
¥	葡萄酒价格：	$ $ $
	酒单酒款数：	14000
	杯卖酒数：	13
¥	杯卖酒价格：	MOP60-150
¥	开瓶费：	MOP400
	酒单撰写人：	Mr. Paul Lo
	电　话：	853 88037788
	营业时间：	11：30-14：30, 18：30-22：30 10：00-15：00（周日及公众假期）
	地　　址：	澳门葡京路新葡京酒店 2 楼
@	网　址：	www.grandlisboahotel.com

荣获《米其林指南 香港 澳门 2014》颁发一星殊荣的"大厨"坐落于新葡京酒店三楼，坐拥澳门优美全景。有别于一般扒房，餐厅将创新概想与传统扒房文化融合，集合日本、澳洲、美国、荷兰等世界各地顶级的牛扒及游水海鲜供即场挑选，于开放式厨房即席烹调。大厨更提供全城最丰富的自助沙律吧、日本寿司吧及自制甜品，为顾客带来全新的扒房感受。

THE KITCHEN
大厨

牛排馆

酒单大奖专家评审团之酒单点评：

"大厨"是新葡京酒店众多餐厅中的一员，酒单非常壮观，今年增长到12700款酒之多。翻阅这么全面地酒单无疑会耗点时间，慢慢来，后面更有令人神往的酒款在等着你。美酒佳酿接踵而至，令人目不暇接啊。

The mega wine list that The Kitchen draws upon as one of a number of restaurants within the Grand Lisboa complex has grown from last year to 12,700 wines. A most complete and time consuming read awaits you! Take your time, an Aladdin's Cave of magical offerings awaits. Icons and gems rub shoulders.

¥	人均消费	MOP 270-1600
¥	葡萄酒价格	$ $ $
♟	酒单酒款数	14000
▽	杯卖酒数	10
¥	杯卖酒价格	MOP 150 - MOP 200
¥	开 瓶 费	MOP 400
☺	酒单撰写人	Mr. Paul Lo
☎	电　　话	853 88037777
⏰	营业时间	12：00 - 14：30,18：30 - 22：30
🏠	地　　址	澳门葡京路新葡京酒店 3 楼
@	网　　址	www.grandlisboahotel.com

"御膳房"连续两年赢得米其林星级荣誉的，主厨 Guillaume Galliot 深信食物的天然真味是美膳的灵魂，巧妙地融会每个小节，引领宾客寻探味觉艺术的精髓，令每个餐飨体验变成一连串的新发现。

THE TASTING ROOM BY GALLIOT
御膳房

法式

酒单大奖专家评审团之酒单点评：

"御膳房"的酒单就好似一本法国和意大利的葡萄酒名品录。我们能感到它对希拉和赤霞珠的偏好，De Beaucastel、莎普蒂尔和吉加乐等酒款让人食欲大增。

The Tasting Room lives up to its name with a stellar wine list that reads like a Who's Who of the French and Italian wine industries. We sense a leaning to syrah and cabernet sauvignon grapes with collections of De Beaucastel, Chapoutier and Guigal particularly mouthwatering.

¥	人均消费：	MOP400-900
¥	葡萄酒价格：	$ $ $
🍷	酒单酒款数：	750
🍷	杯卖酒数：	12
¥	杯卖酒价格：	MOP70-598
¥	开 瓶 费：	MOP400
👤	酒单撰写人：	Mr. Mathieu Gaignon
📞	电 话：	853 88686681
🕐	营业时间：	12：00 - 15：00，18：00 - 23：00
🏠	地 址：	澳门路氹连贯公路新濠天地皇冠度假酒店 3 楼
@	网 址：	www.cityofdreamsmacau.com

　　"紫逸轩"是澳门四季酒店的中餐厅，开业至今一直采用优质食材，配合传统烹调技巧，避免过多调味，保持食物的原汁原味，以表达传统广东菜肴的精粹。每款菜式的设计充分表达厨师们的严谨要求。室内设计由著名的酒店室内设计公司 Hirsch Bender Associates 全程策划。设计师于大厅中央创新地设置了一个华贵的酒窖，珍藏及陈列了来自世界各地顶级名酒，贵宾不但可自行挑选各款佳酿，侍酒师亦可为客人推介与菜式相搭的佳酿。

ZI YAT HEEN
紫逸轩

粤式

酒单大奖专家评审团之酒单点评：

一系列法国佳酿和欧洲他国的美酒撑起这份酒单。一级园中有许多高性价比之作。很高兴看到博若莱和气泡红酒出现在这份酒单上，它们都是粤菜的上选搭配。

An established wine list that confidently presents a range of fine French wines with strong support from Europe. Some of the best value can be found among the Premier Crus. Good to see Beaujolais and sparkling reds embraced, great company for Cantonese cooking.

¥	人均消费	RMB550-850
¥	葡萄酒价格	$ $ $
🍷	酒单酒款数	1200
🍷	杯卖酒数	12
¥	杯卖酒价格	MOP85-240
¥	开瓶费	MOP500
👤	酒单撰写人	Ms. Hedi Lao
📞	电　话	853 28818818
🕐	营业时间	12：00-14：30,18：30-22：30
🏠	地　址	澳门氹仔望德圣母湾四季酒店大堂
@	网　址	www.fourseasons.com/macau

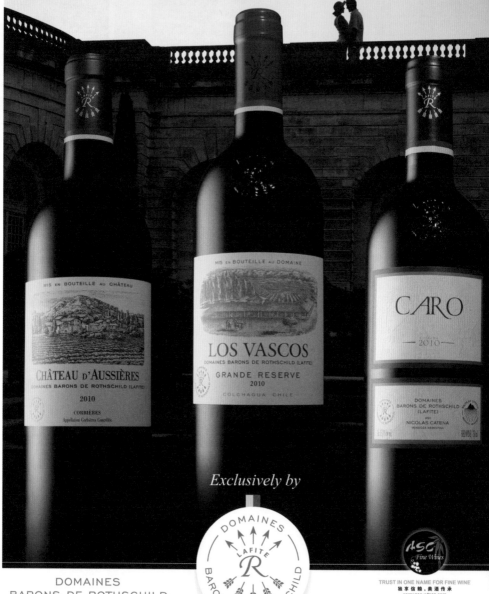

Mr. Dong-Song Wang

西班牙籍主厨 Daniel Negreira 曾在包括 El bulli、Arzak、Mugaritz 在内的多家西班牙米其林三星餐厅历练过，餐厅选用各种新鲜且令人惊艳的食材，以西班牙料理的方式得以呈现。擅长拆解、重组食物元素，并以新式手法呈现，搜索各地创意，从西班牙古老食谱汲取养分，集结多年料理经验，古老与创新、传统与现代、家乡与异地，没有边界、没有形式。餐厅曾被 *The Miele Guide 2010-2011* 评鉴为"台湾最佳餐厅之一"。

D.N INNOVACION

  台湾地区最佳葡萄酒酒单

酒单大奖专家评审团之酒单点评：

这是一份犹如《圣经》一样的酒单！这里处处闪耀着明星酒款，让人不能置信的香槟酒单——45 款库克，其最老的年份酒可以追溯到 1966 年，这怎么可能？！这还不算什么，法国和西班牙顶级酒庄的众多年份酒以及不同系列的酒款让这份酒单熠熠生辉。它对德国酒的选择也同样出色。

What a page turner! All the stars of the wine firmament are here starting with Champagne. How does a range of 45 various Krug wines back to 1966 sound? And it gets better. Multiple vintages and styles from the major wine houses of France and Spain abound. Boasts a strong German presence too.

创新西班牙式

¥	人均消费	TWD2000
¥	葡萄酒价格	$ $ $
🍷	酒单酒款数	1730
🍷	杯卖酒数	15
¥	杯卖酒价格	TWD200-680
¥	开瓶费	TWD500
👤	酒撰写人	Mr. Dong-Song Wang
☎	电　话	886 2 87801155
🕐	营业时间	12：00-15：00,18：00-22：30
🏠	地　址	台北市信义区松仁路 93 号
@	网　址	www.dn-asia.com

在白天，位于 10 楼的 Woobar 是时尚人士洽公、姐妹淘谈心的最佳去处。到了晚上，这里则摇身一变——成为极具风格、炫目迷人的时尚男女聚集地。知名 DJ 让宾客感受音乐魔力，红白沙发与大理石墙上的唇形投影灯更增添了性感的氛围。

WOOBAR

酒单大奖专家评审团之酒单点评：

这是一次短暂的葡萄酒环球之旅，除了停驻在某些商业化的酒庄，还有可选的顶级酒商。在有限的酒款中，新世界酒款数量却占首位，香槟则另外占据一席之地。各种混合的鸡尾酒款让人产生跃跃欲试的想法。

A short tour around the world of wine stopping by some of the more commercial wineries mixed with the high end. Table wines on this tight list tend to be dominated by the New World but Champagne has its own substantial and thorough section. Lab mixology drinks to start look like good fun.

西式

❤	人均消费	TWD700
¥	葡萄酒价格：	$ $
🍾	酒单酒款数：	77
🍷	杯卖酒数：	10
¥	杯卖酒价格：	TWD350-790
¥	开瓶费：	TWD500
👤	酒单撰写人：	Miss Vivian Lin
📞	电　话：	886 2 77038766
🕐	营业时间：	10：00 - 02：00
🏠	地　址：	台北市忠孝东路五段 10 号 10 楼
@	网　址：	www.woobartaipei.com/en

陈岚舒主厨

Mr. Thomas Ho

Le Moût 法文原意为静待发酵成葡萄酒的香醇玉液，表达点滴纯酿、萃取食物精华、追求极致美味，隐含陈岚舒主厨对料理探本求源的精神。以纯正法式烹调，结合台湾这块土地上的丰美与世界各地顶级的食材，坚持法式逻辑的工序与自由奔放的料理创意，让不同文化碰撞出惊人的小致美感。

LE MOÛT RESTAURANT

酒单大奖专家评审团之酒单点评：

侍酒师 Thomas Ho 在酒单上偏爱法国酒。人们就能找到一些性价比更高的佳酿。比如那些产自一级园的酒款，价格合理而且让人唇间留香。走之前一定不要忘记喝上一杯 1957 年份的 Boal。

Sommelier Thomas Ho has built a strong wine list of French wines with emphasis on some of the better value labels. The selection of Premier Crus, for instance, shows a particularly rich seam of gems at fair prices. And you'll definitely want to leave room for the 1957 Boal by the glass!

法式

¥	人均消费：	TWD4000
¥	葡萄酒价格：	$ $ $
	酒单酒款数：	550
	杯卖酒款数：	20
¥	杯卖酒价格：	TWD650-2200
¥	开 瓶 费：	TWD600/ 瓶 (Schott Zwiesel 杯款) TWD1200/ 瓶 (Riedel Sommelier Black Tie 杯款)
	酒单撰写人：	Mr. Thomas Ho
	电 话：	886 4 23753002
	营业时间：	11: 30 -14: 30, 18: 00 -22: 00(周一休)
	地 址：	台中市西区存中街 59 号
@	网 址：	www.lemout.com

'World Class Wine and Spirit Courses for Business and Pleasure'

I-WAY公司介绍

　　埃韦国际贸易（上海）有限公司于2004年成立，致力于高品质的葡萄酒与烈酒教育。近10年的 WSET 教学经验，已经得到广大学员的好评，将近上千名学员从埃韦葡萄酒学校毕业。公司拥有一流的专业团队，为葡萄酒爱好者提供葡萄酒收藏、投资、酒窖管理、葡萄酒旅游等酒类相关服务。

WSET课程开设

1、葡萄酒与烈酒初级课程

2、葡萄酒与烈酒中级课程

3、葡萄酒与烈酒高级课程

4、烈酒初级课程

5、烈酒中级课程

报名热线

Tel: 021-54660333 或

凌小姐（Jessie）：15821471903 /章小姐（Tina）：13917791710

地址：上海市黄浦区局门路550号202室

埃韦官方微信

AIR FRANCE FIRST & BUSINESS CLASS
法国航空 头等舱和商务舱

  最佳国际航空公司酒单

酒单大奖专家评审团之酒单点评：

由侍酒师 Olivier Poussier 负责的酒单一定不会枯燥。这份酒单广泛地选取法国重要产区的佳酿。每瓶入选酒款都广受好评，你应该对它们都充满信心。

You're in good hands when acclaimed sommelier Olivier Poussier composes the carte des vins. This extensive list is a fitting and glorious showcase of French wine spanning the key regions of France. Every wine listed has been carefully appraised so you can be certain of its quality.

酒单撰写人：Mr. Olivier Poussier
网　　址：www.airfrance.com

AIR NEW ZEALAND BUSINESS PREMIER CLASS
新西兰航空 豪华公务舱

酒单大奖专家评审团之酒单点评：

优质的新西兰葡萄酒齐聚一堂。这里既有耳熟能详的名字，比如 Cloudy Bay 和 Villa Maria，也有待人发掘的酒款。这个包含众多产区和酒商的指南能让您在落地之时成为名副其实的专家。

Take delight in the glorious spread of quality New Zealand wines. Recognisable names, such as Cloudy Bay and Villa Maria, sit alongside lesser-known small producers – so there's plenty to discover. The comprehensive regional and producer guide will make you an expert by the time you land.

酒单撰写人：Miss Kate Radburnd
网　　址：www.airnewzealand.com

BRITISH AIRWAYS FIRST CLASS
英国航空 头等舱

酒单大奖专家评审团之酒单点评：

毫无疑问，在这些酒款陪伴下的旅途会很有趣。顶级产区、明星酒庄、优质年份都是亮点。每款酒都附上平添几分乐趣的简单介绍。从优质香槟到勃艮第和波尔多，最后以苏岱或波特酒收尾。真是极好的旅程。

There's no doubt you'll enjoy your flight with quality wines like these. Premier regions, respected producers and good vintages. Lengthy descriptions for each wine simply add to the pleasure. Start with fine Champagne, move onto Burgundy and Bordeaux end with Sauternes or Port. Superb.

酒单撰写人：Mr. Christopher Cole
网　　址：www.ba.com

EMIRATES FIRST CLASS
阿联酋航空 头等舱

酒单大奖专家评审团之酒单点评：

简洁而不简单的酒款让您的旅途不再无聊。以香槟王年份酒作开胃酒，接下来选一款澳大利亚、新西兰或者法国的白葡萄酒，然后右岸红或者澳大利亚的西拉子也可以成为红葡萄酒类的备选。最后用苏岱或 40 年的波特酒做结束吧。

A succinct selection of well-chosen wines guaranteed to help you enjoy your fight. Start with vintage Dom Perignon before sampling fine Australian, New Zealand and French whites. Right bank reds and Australian shiraz on offer in the reds. Finish with sauternes or a 40 year old port!

酒单撰写人：Mr. Robin Padgett
网　　址：www.emirates.com

GARUDA INDONESIA BUSINESS & FIRST CLASS
印尼航空 商务舱和头等舱

酒单大奖专家评审团之酒单点评：

精选法国经典产区的佳酿，包括两款 2000 年份的香槟。优质的夏瑟尼 - 蒙哈榭和现代的澳大利亚霞多丽是新旧产区的典型代表。在落地之前，请试试玛歌或者老年份的巴萨克。

A strong selection from the classic regions of France including two Champagnes from the 2000 vintage. Compare old and new by tasting a fine Chassagne-Montrachet alongside a comtemporary Australian Chardonnay – both excellent examples of their type. End with Margaux or aged Barsac prior to landing.

网　　址：www.garuda-indonesia.com.cn

SCANDANAVIAN AIRLINES - BUSINESS CLASS
北欧航空 商务舱

酒单大奖专家评审团之酒单点评：

著名的英国酒评家和电视评论员 Oz Clarke 为北欧航空提供了酒单建议，这里都是知名产区的佳酿，尽是您所期望的有深度的珍品。

Renowned UK-based wine critic and television presenter Oz Clarke offers his selection on board the friendly skies of Scandinavian Airlines, a best-of of available wines from prominent international wine regions. Great depth in the tasting notes, as expected!

酒单撰写人：Mr. Oz Clark
酒单酒款数：12
网　　址：www.flysas.com

SINGAPORE AIRLINES SUITE / FIRST CLASS
新加坡航空 套房和头等舱

酒单大奖专家评审团之酒单点评：

精致即是美！精挑细选的酒款包括香槟里响当当的 Krug 和香槟王、顶级勃艮第和波尔多、托斯卡纳俄罗斯河谷以及摩泽尔的珍宝。酒单以淡雅脱俗的形式呈现，每款酒都有详尽的介绍。

Small is beautiful. Nine expertly chosen wines - Grand Marque Champagnes such as Krug and Dom Perignon, top Burgundy and Bordeaux, plus gems from Tuscany, Russian River Valley and the Mosel. The presentation of the list is elegant and refined and includes extensive descriptions for each wine.

酒单撰写人：Miss Jeannie Cho Lee
网　　址：www.singaporeair.com

COMITÉ
CHAMPAGNE

真正的香槟酒
只来自于法国香槟地区

CHAMPAGNE only comes from
CHAMPAGNE, France

http://www.champagne-civc.cn/

100 CENTURY AVENUE, PARK HYATT SHANGHAI ♥♥♥

100 Century AvenuePudong New Area, Shanghai 200120
+86 21 68881234
http://shanghai.park.hyatt.com
Cuisine: Western & Chinese
Wine list by Mr Adrian Zhang & Mr Jean-Marc Nolant
Wine on list: 490 (36 by the glass)
Wine prices: $$$
By the glass: RMB 110 - RMB 480

This list celebrates the diversity of the world of wine, with wines arranged by colour, then variety, country and region. Quality is high across the board, with attention paid to the inclusion of sustainably produced wine. The by-the-glass offering is stunning, with over 35 wines available.

121 BC ♥♥

42-44 Peel Street, Soho, Hong Kong
852 23950200
www.121bc.com.hk
Cuisine: Italian
Wine list by Mr Simone Sammuri
Wine on list: 120 (20 by the glass)
Wine prices: $$
By the glass: HKD 60 - HKD 125

 Winner Best Wine Bar List

Small, modest in price and aspirations, 121 BC just might be showing the way for a future in Hong Kong dining where size isn't everything. We applaud the 100 per cent focus on Italian wines and the number of interesting wines by the glass from some of the quieter, smaller producers going.

28 HUBIN ROAD, HYATT REGENCY HANGZHOU ♥♥

28 Hu Bin Road, Hangzhou, Zhejiang 310006
+86 571 8779 1234
hangzhou.regency.hangzhou.cn
Cuisine: Hangzhou
Wine list by Mr Jan Stoverink
Wine on list: 163 (26 by the glass)
Wine prices: $$$

A sophisticated list to match the refined and beautiful Hangzhou dishes served at this highly respected restaurant. The astute selection of Australian and New Zealand wines sit comfortably alongside old world classics, mainly French. The by-the-glass is satisfying.

29 GRILL RESTAURANT, CONRAD BEIJING ♥♥

29 North Dongsahuan, Chaoyang District, Beijing 100027
+86 1065846300
beijing.conradhotels.com
Cuisine: Western
Wine list by Mr Remi Torres
Wine on list: 180 (17 by the glass)
Wine prices: $$

An excellent by-the-glass list traverses the globe and some very fine, less-seen producers, while the body of the list manages to delight with all-corners-of-globe exploration of fine wine producing regions. Alto Adige to a neatly chosen selection of Bordeaux and some fancy Champagne are highlights.

8 1/2 OTTO E MEZZO BOMBANA HONG KONG ♥♥

Shop 202 Landmark Alexandra, Central, Hong Kong
+852 2537 8859
www.ottoemezzobombana.com
Cuisine: Italian
Wine list by Mr Antonio Bombini
Wine on list: 687 (31 by the glass)
Wine prices: $$$
By the glass: HKD 90 - HKD 440

The wines of Italy play tag with those of France throughout this enthusiastic wine list but the Italians win outright with a greater depth of selections led by Piedmonte and Tuscany. Wines by the glass are particularly appealing supported by a thorough half bottle/magnums collection.

8 1/2 OTTO E MEZZO BOMBANA SHANGHAI ♥♥♥

6th floor, Associate Mission Building, No. 169, Yuanmingyuan Road, Huangpu District, Shanghai 200002
021-60872890
www.ottoemezzobombana.com/shanghai
Cuisine: Italian Fine Dining
Wine list by Mr Gian Luca Fusetto
Wine on list: 500 (18 by the glass)
Wine prices: $$$
By the glass: RMB 90 - RMB 450

 Winner Best Selection of One Country's Wine

A dazzling showcase of all things Italian – from the sumptuous décor to the superb menu and glittering wine list. There are feature pages for elite Italian producers, with back vintages of top wines plus a selection of magnums. While most countries are represented, the focus is undeniably Italian.

AGUA ♟

4/F Nali Patio, 81 Sanlitun North Street, Chaoyang, Beijing 100027
86-10-5208-6188
www.aqua.com.hk
Cuisine: Spanish
Wine list by Mr Marc Font
Wine on list: 94 (12 by the glass)
Wine prices: $
By the glass: RMB 70 - RMB 95

The food menu is of course Spanish so there's no disappointment in seeing the breadth of Spain heavily represented in this list. There's lots of diversity in Spanish styles and a smattering of international interlopers for good measure. Great choices for cuisine, with fine wines also in the mix.

AIR FRANCE FIRST / BUSINESS CLASS ♟ ♟ ♟

Room 1602, 16/FBuilding 3China Overseas Plaza, Chaoyang, Beijing 100026
1059220809
www.airfrance.com
Cuisine: Airline
Wine list by Mr Olivier Poussier

 Winner Best International Airline Wine List

You're in good hands when acclaimed sommelier Olivier Poussier composes the carte des vins. This extensive list is a fitting and glorious showcase of French wine spanning the key regions of France. Every wine listed has been carefully appraised so you can be certain of its quality.

AIR NEW ZEALAND BUSINESS PREMIER CLASS, AIR NEW ZEALAND ♟ ♟

3701, The Center 989 Chang Le Road , Shanghai 200031
8602151097070
www.airnewzealand.com
Cuisine: Airline
Wine list by Miss Kate Radburnd

Take delight in the glorious spread of quality New Zealand wines. Recognisable names, such as Cloudy Bay and Villa Maria, sit alongside lesser-known small producers – so there's plenty to discover. The comprehensive regional and producer guide will make you an expert by the time you land.

ALFIE'S ♟ ♟

Alfred Dunhill StoreM/F, Shop M18-19Landmark Prince's Building10 Chater Road, Central, Hong Kong
852 25304422
http://www.dunhill.com/the-homes/hong-kong/
Cuisine: British
Wine on list: 172 (9 by the glass)
Wine prices: $$
By the glass: HKD 90 - HKD 150

This smart wine list is compiled with assistance from the Sarment wine buying/management group and contains some real finds such as Garagiste (Aus), Jacques Picard (Fr) as well as a smashing grouping of Premier Crus. Prices are fair and there's plenty of new discovery for wine lovers.

AQUA ROMA/AQUA TOKYO ♟

29th Floor, 1 Peking Road, Tsim Sha Tsui, Hong Kong
+852 3427 2288
www.aqua.com.hk
Cuisine: Italian & Japanese
Wine list by Mr Bartlomiej Szyniec
Wine on list: 300 (22 by the glass)
Wine prices: $$$
By the glass: HKD 98 - HKD 138

Italian and Japanese food and wine together? That's a hard act to follow with wine but Aqua Roma gives the idea its best shot with a wine list angled mainly towards the former. Some nice, all-round quality Italian wines can be found. A small but tidy listing of sake follows.

ARIA RESTAURANT, CHINA WORLD HOTEL ♟ ♟

No.1 Jianguomenwai Avenue, Beijing 100004
(8610)65052266-5743
www.shangri-la.com
Cuisine: Modern European
Wine list by Mr Gary Zhang
Wine on list: 514 (28 by the glass)
Wine prices: $$$
By the glass: RMB 95 - RMB 230

Anywhere that pours JJ Prum riesling by-the-glass will instantly win friends, then the list cascades into a who's who of top-end wine producers and marquee wines. Dom Perignon "Oenotheque" 1976 a start, but great listings of Bordeaux and Burgundy follow. Broad selection of excellent wines here.

AURORA, ALTIRA HOTEL

Level 10, Altira HotelAvenida de Kwong Tung, Taipa, Macau
(853) 8803 6622
www.altiramacau.com
Cuisine: Authentic Italian
Wine list by Mr Keith Lam
Wine on list: 650 (18 by the glass)
Wine prices: $$$
By the glass: MOP 80 - MOP 160

A near faultless wine list that pulses with quality and iconic wine names. Highly mouthwatering! It starts with a Bang! with a vertical of Latour (1945-2005) and what follows is a game of tag between France and Italy and the rest of the world. The drinker wins. Half bottles and magnums aplenty too.

AUX BEAUX ARTS, MGM MACAU

Avenida Dr. Sun Yat Sen, Nape, Macau
85388028888
www.mgmmacau.com
Cuisine: French
Wine list by Mr Adolphus Foo
Wine on list: 1450 (14 by the glass)
Wine prices: $$$
By the glass: MOP 45 - MOP 220

A magnum opus! A wine list six years in the making that reflects the beautiful, the iconic, the solid gold performers and the strangely eclectic. A Japanese sparkling wine anyone? If one should reach the end, the temptation of wine alliances with Palace Bacaco, Famille Becot and Luis Pato await.

BAROLO, THE RITZ-CARLTON, BEIJING

83A Jian Guo Road, China Central Place, Chaoyang District, Beijing 100025
86-10-59088151
http://www.ritzcarlton.com/en/Properties/Beijing/Default.htm
Cuisine: Italian
Wine list by Mr Larry Yang
Wine on list: 500 (0 by the glass)
Wine prices: $$$
By the glass: RMB 80 - RMB 398

A jaw-dropping selection of vintage Bordeaux stretching back to the 1950s is a highlight, but the epic Sommeliers Collection is equal to task with great wines of the world. This is a lengthy list of quality and global awareness, fine-tuned to the delightful food menu. A list to pore over.

BELLE-VUE, GRAND HYATT SHENZHEN

1881 Baoan Nan Road, Luohu District, Shenzhen, Guangdong 518001
+86 755 82661234
www.shenzhen.grand.hyatt.com
Cuisine: European
Wine list by Ms Van Leeuwen Stijin
Wine on list: 131 (17 by the glass)
Wine prices: $$

This wine list packs in a lot for a shorter line-up; high quality Champagne leads the way, and a selection of premier wine regions follow. The by-the-glass selection is also inspiring, with just under 20 wines on offer, from fine wine producers around the winemaking world. A well-honed list .

BELON, BANYAN TREE MACAU

Galaxy Macau Resort, Avenida Marginal Flor de Lotus, Cotai, Macau
+853 8883 8833
http://www.banyantree.com/en/macau/
Cuisine: European
Wine list by Mr Andy Tam
Wine on list: 197 (11 by the glass)
Wine prices: $$$
By the glass: MOP 90 - MOP 218

Just as you can order Dover sole, Norwegian mackerel, Colorado lamb and Chilean sea bass off the food menu here, expect a similarly expansive world wine list. Even a Thai syrah gets a listing! Big names abound, at big prices, but there are also some star finds along with an excellent fizz component.

BISCOTTI, SOFITEL JINAN SLIVER PLAZA

No. 66 Luoyuan Avenue, Jinan, Shandong 250063
0531-86068888
www.sofitel.com/2875
Cuisine: Italian
Wine list by Mr Bob Wu
Wine on list: 118 (22 by the glass)
Wine prices: $

A cheerful list that shows best assets of the most well-known wine regions of the world, from a couple of stunning First Growths to premium Champagne and examples from USA, South Africa and China for those seeking further interest. Italian wines of course get time to shine with the food menu too.

Brasserie 1893, Waldorf Astoria Beijing

5-15 Jinyu Hutong, Dongcheng District, Beijing 100006
861085208989
http://waldorfastoria3.hilton.com/en/hotels/china/waldorf-astoria-beijing-BJSWAWA/index.html
Cuisine: Western
Wine list by Mr Pieter Ham
Wine on list: 359 (21 by the glass)
Wine prices: $$
By the glass: RMB 85 - RMB 195

It seems the list focuses on quality rather than affordable wines, and therefore showcases some of the great producers of the world. Of particular interest is the depth of Spanish wine and rare wines of Loire and Burgundy, with chardonnay a hero on this menu. There's plenty to relish here.

British Airways First Class

Room 180518/f, Tower B, Winterless Center1 West Dawang Rd, Chaoyang, Beijing 10020
861065388672
www.ba.com
Cuisine: Airline
Wine list by Mr Christopher Cole

There's no doubt you'll enjoy your flight with quality wines like these. Premier regions, respected producers and good vintages. Lengthy descriptions for each wine simply add to the pleasure. Start with fine Champagne, move onto Burgundy and Bordeaux end with Sauternes or Port. Superb.

Burdigala

301 Jiashan Lu, Xuhui, Shanghai 200031
021 6422 9826
http://www.theburdigala.com/
Cuisine: French Bistro
Wine list by Mr Franck Boudot
Wine on list: 70 (7 by the glass)
Wine prices: $$
By the glass: RMB 45 - RMB 65

Bordeaux in China is often priced beyond the reach of the average wine lover. So it's refreshing to see this modern French bistro promoting some affordable, lesser-known appellations and styles, as well as respected grand cru classes. A visit to the adjoining wine store is a must.

C Grill & Wine Bar

31 Renmin Road East, Zhongshan District, Dalian, Liaoning 116001
+86 0411 8677 6666
conradhotels.com.cn/dalian
Cuisine: French
Wine list by Mr Marco Ma
Wine on list: 152 (85 by the glass)
Wine prices: $$
By the glass: RMB 50 - RMB 280

Hard to not like a list that starts with 'Unforgettable' wine selections then follows up with some of the grandest wines of Champagne, Burgundy, Bordeaux, Australia and Spain. Beyond the fancier wines are some thoughtful listings of emerging and lesser-known wines. Well balanced list.

Cachet - All Day Dining, The Langham

No. 99, Madang Road, Xintiandi, Shanghai 200021
86 21 2330 2288
xintiandi.langhamhotels.com
Cuisine: International
Wine list by Mr Michael Zhang
Wine on list: 69 (11 by the glass)
Wine prices: $$

This list has almost doubled from last year but it's good to see its strong inner core of world class wines from the most reliable names in the business remains. Names like J.J.Prum, Felton Road, Peter Lehmann and Duval-Leroy are always welcome. Pop into the Premium Cellar list for star finds.

Calypso, Jing An Shangri-La Hotel

1218 Middle Yan'an Road, Jing An Kerry Centre, West Nanjing Road, Shanghai 200040
86 21 22038888
www.jinganshangdining.com
Cuisine: Mediterranean
Wine list by Mr Jerry Liao
Wine on list: 110 (19 by the glass)
Wine prices: $$
By the glass: RMB 70 - RMB 120

This modern list is in step with the restaurant's bright, airy surrounds and contemporary Mediterranean menu. Whites are classified in the flower, fruit or mineral spectrum while reds are organised varietally. There's a kaleidoscope of well-priced wines from around the globe plus the odd icon.

CAMELIA, FOUR SEASONS HOTEL PUDONG, SHANGHAI ♈♈♈

210 Century Avenue, Pudong, Shanghai 200120
8621 20361300
http://www.fourseasons.com/pudong/dining/restaurants/camelia
Cuisine: French
Wine list by Miss Ying Guo
Wine on list: 260 (16 by the glass)
Wine prices: $$$
By the glass: RMB 90 - RMB 190

       Winner Best Hotel Restaurant Wine List
       Winner Best Aperitif List
       Winner Best Digestif List
       Finalist

A mere glimpse is all that's needed to see there's an expert at the helm. Sommelier Ying Guo presents an inspirational list, full of the brightest stars of the wine world – from famous icons to boutique gems. Regionality is taken seriously to ensure a true global experience is offered.

CANTON RESTAURANT, THE VENETIAN HOTEL RESORT HOTEL ♈♈

Estrada da Baia deN. Senhora da Esperanca s/n, Taipa, Macau
85381189930
www.venetianmacao.com
Cuisine: Chinese Cantonese
Wine list by Mr Jimmy Valentine
Wine on list: 592 (8 by the glass)
Wine prices: $$$
By the glass: MOP 40 - MOP 210

What's your drink? There are plenty of options here from Bordeaux First Growths and Italian Barolos through to some economical Aussie and Spanish reds and whites. Special occasion wines are a specialty. How about a '82 Lafite for AU$9990 or MOP72,000? The odd gem can also be found.

CAPITAL M ♈

3/F, No.2 Qianmen Pedestrian Street(just south of Tian'anmen Square), Beijing 100051
8610 6702-2727
http://www.m-restaurantgroup.com/capitalm/home.html
Cuisine: Modern European
Wine list by Mr Zi Zheng Xu
Wine on list: 300 (20 by the glass)
Wine prices: $$
By the glass: RMB 60 - RMB 140

Divided into 'short list' and 'long list', this innovative wine menu has a decided leaning to what could be considered 'New World' producers. Highlights however are great Champagne and some excellent Australian boutique producers. As a bonus wines are available by selected glass and carafe too.

CATALUNYA ♈♈

G/F Guardian House32 Oi Kwan Road, Wan Chai, Hong Kong
+852 2866 7900
www.catalunya.hk
Cuisine: Spanish
Wine list by Mr Miquel Sabrià
Wine on list: 400 (10 by the glass)
Wine prices: $$
By the glass: HKD 88 - HKD 158

Ah, Catalunya . . . the home of Cava. Expect to drink Spanish sparkling and a whole lot of Spanish blue bloods here. Look no further than wines by the glass for a good introduction to Spain at fair prices. This unpretentious all-rounder looks outside Spain too, offering the odd gem.

CATCH, FOUR SEASONS HOTEL GUANGZHOU ♈

5 Zhujiang West Road, Pearl River New City,Tianhe District, Guangzhou, Guangdong 510623
8620 8883-3300
http://www.fourseasons.com/guangzhou/dining/restaurants/catch/
Cuisine: Western / Seafood
Wine list by Mr Jackie Zhang
Wine on list: 1 (17 by the glass)
Wine prices: $
By the glass: RMB 88 - RMB 158

There's some great consideration in the food and wine matching suggestions which works as a good indication for the quality of wine to follow. Excellent Champagne selection, producers like Jaboulet and Gaja, and a broad global outlook on wine, make this an attractive list.

CATHAY ROOM, FAIRMONT PEACE HOTEL ♈♈

No. 20, East Nanjing Rd, Shanghai 200002
86 21
www.fairmont.com/peace-hotel-shanghai
Cuisine: European
Wine list by Mr Eddy Shi
Wine on list: 250 (20 by the glass)
Wine prices: $$$
By the glass: RMB 69 - RMB 229

A contemporary European-flavoured wine list that stars a strong selection of the ever reliable and the familiar. The wines by the glass listing and the presence of a goodly number of Chinese wines to be applauded. Older vintages are also a feature.

CEPE RESTAURANT, THE RITZ-CARLTON BEIJING, FINANCIAL STREET ♟

1 Jin Cheng Fang Street East, Financial Street, Xicheng
District, Beijing 100033
(86 10) 6601 6666
www.ritzcarlton.com/hotels/beijing_financial
Cuisine: Italian
Wine list by Mr Daniel Deng
Wine on list: 356 (22 by the glass)
Wine prices: $$
By the glass: RMB 88 - RMB 398

*Impressive focus on Italian wines found in this list, and wholly
appropriate considering the cuisines of the restaurant. Wine
lovers will no doubt enjoy the lengthy cellar list of Angelo
Gaja's magnificent wines, though there's plenty of stars
throughout the list. Wines of France are also impressive.*

CHAR, HOTEL INDIGO SHANGHAI ON THE BUND ♟

29f, 585 Zhong Shan Dong Er Rd(near Dongmen Rd),
Shanghai 200010
+86 21 33029995
www.char-thebund.com
Cuisine: Steakhouse
Wine list by Mr Barthélémy Lee
Wine on list: 100 (12 by the glass)
Wine prices: $$
By the glass: RMB 90 - RMB 160

*The honesty of both the menu and wine list makes this an
endearing favourite of locals and visitors alike, not to mention
the stunning views. Wines are grouped by style to make
selection easier, with a fair spread from France and Australia.
15 by the glass.*

CHEZ PATRICK RESTAURANT ♟ ♟

2?F GardenEast222 Queen's Road East, Wan Chai, Hong Kong
852 2541 1401
www.chezpatrick.hk
Cuisine: French
Wine list by Mr Patrick Goubier
Wine on list: 75 (10 by the glass)
Wine prices: $$
By the glass: HKD 80 - HKD 180

*A most charming small wine list of just 75 wines full of interest
and fantastic value for money.It remains focussed on French
wines with some delicious medium priced examples from
quality producers like Meo Camuzet, Jadot and Certan de May.
Aged wines mingle with fresh youngsters. Lots to like here.*

CUISINE CUISINE, THE MIRA HONG KONG ♟

3/F, The Mira Hong Kong, 118 Nathan Road, Tsimshatsui,
Kowloon, Hong Kong
(852)2315 5222
www.themirahotel.com
Cuisine: Cantonese
Wine list by Mr Alan Sun
Wine on list: 365 (12 by the glass)
Wine prices: $$
By the glass: HKD 95 - HKD 2125

*A smart Cantonese food menu is well supported by a world
wine listing full of familiar wine names. The list will be
reassuring to those who love the iconic producers of both the
New and Old Worlds. Sadly, no Chinese wine producers have
yet come on board.*

D.N INNOVACION ♟ ♟ ♟

93 Songren Rd, Xinyi District, Taipei, Taiwan 110
+886 (2) 8780 1155
www.dn-asia.com
Cuisine: Spainish Innovation
Wine list by Mr Dong-Song Wang
Wine on list: 1730 (15 by the glass)
Wine prices: $$$
By the glass: TWD 200 - TWD 680

 Winner Best Wine List – Taiwan

*What a page turner! All the stars of the wine firmament are
here starting with Champagne. How does a range of 45 various
Krug wines back to 1966 sound? And it gets better. Multiple
vintages and styles from the major wine houses of France and
Spain abound. Boasts a strong German presence too.*

DA VINCI RESTAURANT, SHANGRI-LA HOTEL, QINGDAO ♟

9 Xiang Gang Zhong Lu, Qingdao, Shandong 266071
(86 532) 8388 3838
www.shangri-la.com
Cuisine: Italian
Wine list by Mr Steven Yin
Wine on list: 118 (19 by the glass)
Wine prices: $

*It's great to see wine from China getting some space on this list
alongside luminaries from Burgundy, USA and Italy. It's not a
long list, but it is well chosen and works very well with the
cuisines and offers broad selection from around the world.
Something for everyone.*

DACCAPO, REGENT BEIJING ♟
99 Jinbao Street, Dongcheng District, Beijing 100005
86 10 85221888
http://www.regenthotels.com/EN/Beijing
Cuisine: Italian
Wine list by Mr Richard Pirsch
Wine on list: 56 (6 by the glass)
Wine prices: $$
By the glass: RMB 60 - RMB 1000

The list is set decidedly to the premium; lengthy in big name wines like Henschke's Hill Of Grace, Solaia and Bollinger RD (1997 and 1999!) making this an impressive and fancy wine offering. There's less in the easy-drinking section but what's been selected is undoubtedly worthy too.

DINING ROOM, PARK HYATT NINGBO RESORT AND SPA ♟
188 Danyan Road, Dong Qian Lake, Ningbo, Zhejiang 315123
86 574 28881234
ningbo.park.hyatt.com
Cuisine: Western and Chinese
Wine on list: 24 (5 by the glass)
Wine prices: $$
By the glass: RMB 90 - RMB 150

It's not a huge list, but there's thoughtful selection that sees not only new and old world producers listed, but some of their best regional assets, like zinfandel of California or Marlborough pinot noir. Confidently curated. Aperitif and digestif listings are an impressive and lengthy highlight.

DON ALFONSO 1890 ♟ ♟ ♟
3/F, Grand Lisboa Hotel, Avenida de Lisboa, Macau
(853) 8803 7722
www.grandlisboahotel.com
Cuisine: Southern Italian
Wine on list: 12780 (8 by the glass)
Wine prices: $$$
By the glass: MOP 130 - MOP 200

Another list drawing from the vast cellar of the Grand Hotel Lisboa. In keeping with the cuisine, skip to the Italian reds and choose from pages of Piedmontese and Tuscan glories. The Italian white selection is comparatively small (though the tempting list of white Burgundy is seemingly endless!).

DONGHAI 88, HYATT REGENCY QINGDAO ♟ ♟
88 Donghai East Road, Qingdao, Shandong 266061
+86 532 8612 1234
http://qingdao.regency.hyatt.com/
Cuisine: Chinese
Wine list by Mr Michal Krauze
Wine on list: 114 (8 by the glass)
Wine prices: $$
By the glass: RMB 55 - RMB 130

 Winner Best Beer List

The wine list is very well appointed with fine producers and exceptional wines, with Bordeaux and Burgundy starring, but the real surprise is the exceptional beer listing, which shows impressively including excellent Trappist and Abbey brews. Spirits are also lengthy in listing. Creative list here.

DUKE'S, THE LANGHAM, SHENZHEN ♟ ♟
7888 Shennan Boulevard, Futian District, Shenzhen, Guangdong 518040
86-0755-88289888
shenzhen.langhamhotels.com
Cuisine: Western
Wine list by Miss Julia Zhu
Wine on list: 393 (21 by the glass)
Wine prices: $$
By the glass: RMB 65 - RMB 195

A serious list that offers some of the world's greats, from Domaine de la Romanee Conti to vintage Chateau Musar, and back to premium Australian wines, with an impressive selection of mature and young wines covering a great breadth of fine wine regions. By the glass showcases some premium wines too.

DYNASTY 8, CONRAD HOTEL ♟ ♟
Level 1, Conrad MacaoSands Cotai Central Cotai Trip, Taipa, Macau
+853 8113 8920
macau.dynasty8.reservation@conradhotels.com
Cuisine: Chinese
Wine list by Mr Arnaud Echalier
Wine on list: 501 (18 by the glass)
Wine prices: $$$
By the glass: MOP 30 - MOP 165

A wine list that plays to the Chinese wine lover's interest in Bordeaux and cabernet sauvignon. Most of the big Bordeaux names are here. However, look outside France and there's plenty to enjoy. Good value can be found in second labels from known producers.

EBONY, MANDARIN ORIENTAL

389 Tianhe Road, Tianhe District, Guangzhou, Guangdong
510620
+86 20 3808 8888
www.mandarinoriental.com
Cuisine: Grill
Wine list by Mr Eric Blomeyer
Wine on list: 321 (12 by the glass)
Wine prices: $$$
By the glass: RMB 120 - RMB 480

★ Winner Best Wine List – Southern China

Any list that starts with bottles of '96 Krug Clos du Ambonnay or '92 Dom Pérignon Oenothèque Rosé is setting a certain high standard, and this menu continues with the hits from premier producers and regions. Encyclopaedic feel to this wine offering, across the wine-growing world. Very impressive.

ELEMENTS, SOFITEL-WANDA-HARBIN

68 Ganshui roadXiangfang District, Harbin, Heilongjiang
150090
+86 451 82336888
www.sofitel.com
Cuisine: French
Wine list by Mr Louis Frank
Wine on list: 115 (26 by the glass)
Wine prices: $

For a medium-sized list it sure does flex its by-the-glass muscles, with just under 30 wines on offer and from across the whole spectrum of wine regions and styles of the list. The wine list feels friendly and accessible, with lots of aromatic whites and medium bodied reds friendly with the cuisine.

YONG FOO ELITE

200 Yung Fu Rd, Jin An District, Shanghai 200031
5466 2727
www.yongfooelite.com/
Cuisine: Shanghaiese
Wine list by Mr Ian Dai
Wine on list: 116 (8 by the glass)
Wine prices: $$$
By the glass: RMB 60 - RMB 190

 Winner Best Club Wine List

French wines dominate the list, particularly top end Burgundy and Bordeaux. Though if looking for something other than a left bank icon or a Cote de Nuits star, then there are a handful of Spanish, Italian and Australian wines worth a look. The red selection trumps the whites.

EMIRATES FIRST CLASS

Room 2707-2710, Tower OneKerry Everbright City218 Tian Mu Road West, Shanghai 200070
2163532288
www.emirates.com
Cuisine: Airline
Wine list by Mr Robin Padgett

A succinct selection of well-chosen wines guaranteed to help you enjoy your fight. Start with vintage Dom Perignon before sampling fine Australian, New Zealand and French whites. Right bank reds and Australian shiraz on offer in the reds. Finish with sauternes or a 40 year old port!

eYAN

No.18 Yingfangli,Gulou District, Fuzhou, Fujian 350001
+86 591 87760519
www.grace-vineyard.com
Cuisine: French & Italian
Wine on list: 121 (14 by the glass)
Wine prices: $$
By the glass: RMB 38 - RMB 88

The Grace Vineyard restaurant wine list highlights the quality produce of this established Chinese wine producer. A wonderful way to better know the wines of China. There's plenty of choose from either by the glass or bottle. Prices are reasonable.

FEAST, SHERATON HUZHOU HOT SPRING RESORT

5858 Taihu Road, Huzhou, Zhejiang 313000
86 572 2299999
www.sheraton.com
Cuisine: French
Wine list by Mr Fankie Lui
Wine on list: 154 (32 by the glass)
Wine prices: $$

While the list showcases some of the world's great wine regions, and a depth of premier producers, it's the lengthy listing of local Chinese wines supported by excellent Chinese rice wine and 'Bai Jui' Liqueurs, that adds an extra 'x-factor'. A great exploration.

FIFTY 8° GRILL, MANDARIN ORIENTAL PUDONG ♟ ♟ ♟

111 Pudong Road (S), Pudong, Shanghai 200120
86212082938
http://www.mandarinoriental.com/shanghai/
Cuisine: French
Wine list by Mr Stephane Builard
Wine on list: 26 (314 by the glass)
Wine prices: $$$
By the glass: RMB 65 - RMB 400

Francophiles will delight in the fine French food and the refined surrounds. The wine list focuses on the classics – plenty of Champagne, Burgundy and Bordeaux – you'll also find some lovely Rhones plus some affordable picks from the south. 26 wines by-the-glass. Balanced international selection.

FLINT GRILL & BAR, JW MARRIOTT HOTEL HONG KONG ♟ ♟

Pacific Place, 88 Queensway, Hong Kong , Hong Kong
852 2810 8366
http://www.marriott.com/hotel-restaurants/hkgdt-jw-marriott-hotel-hong-kong/flint-grill-&-bar/5524699/home-page.mi
Cuisine: Grill
Wine list by Mr Kevin Yung
Wine on list: 146 (19 by the glass)
Wine prices: $$
By the glass: HKD 85 - HKD 388

Flint Bar and Grill boasts 146 seats and 146 wines. Nice synergy! The wine list gives equal time to wine styles from the Old and New Worlds with a particularly envy-worthy grouping of smart Burgundies. Vintages tend to be on the fresher side. Try the Signature Cocktails to start.

FRANCK BISTROT ♟ ♟

Ferguson Lane. 376 Wukang Road, Shanghai 200031
86 (21) 64376465
www.franck.com.cn
Cuisine: French Bistrot
Wine list by Mr Franck Pecol
Wine on list: 260 (11 by the glass)
Wine prices: $$
By the glass: RMB 75 - RMB 140

Take a journey through the regions of France with this refreshingly original selection of French wine. Top-quality producers are at ease alongside little-known artisans and natural wine producers. A menu reflecting the mood and produce of the day makes this an utterly charming place to dine.

G RESTAURANT & BAR, GRAND HYATT GUANGZHOU ♟

12 Zhujiang W. Rd, Pearl River New City, Tianhe District, Guangzhou, Guangdong 510623
+86 20 8396 1234
www.guangzhou.grand.hyatt.com
Cuisine: Western
Wine list by Mr Cristiano Luk
Wine on list: 225 (18 by the glass)
Wine prices: $$
By the glass: RMB 88 - RMB 280

If you've got an eye for good Bordeaux, then you'll find yourself hard-pressed skipping the lengthy pages dedicated to reds of the famed region. That being said, cameos from benchmark Australian, Italian, USA and Burgundy wines also rate highly. A serious list. Don't miss the single malts either!

GARDEN BISTRO, SOFITEL DONGGUAN ROYAL LAGOON ♟ ♟

8 Ying Bin Road Dong Cheng District, Dongguan, Guangdong 523129
+86(0)76922698888
www.sofitel.com
Cuisine: Western
Wine list by Mr Lip Chai Lim
Wine on list: 212 (60 by the glass)
Wine prices: $$

The Western style menu covers a lot of ground. So too, does the wine list sprinkled with a smattering of French and Italian, North and South American and Australasian.For a quick dash around all of them look to the wine flights. What fun! Aged wines a feature here.

GARUDA INDONESIA BUSINESS & FIRST CLASS ♟ ♟

209-210, 2F China Life Tower16 Chaowai St, Chaoyang, Beijing 10020
1085253339
www.garuda-indonesia.com.cn
Cuisine: Airline

A strong selection from the classic regions of France including two Champagnes from the 2000 vintage. Compare old and new by tasting a fine Chassagne-Montrachet alongside a comtemporary Australian Chardonnay – both excellent examples of their type. End with Margaux or aged Barsac prior to landing.

GLAMOUR BAR ♟

6/F, No.5 The Bund (corner of Guangdong Lu), Shanghai 200002
021-63509988
http://www.m-glamour.com/home.html
Cuisine: Lounge Bar
Wine on list: 68 (32 by the glass)
Wine prices: $$
By the glass: RMB 68 - RMB 199

Plenty to like at this chic and sassy Shanghai bar. An international spread of well-known wines, including 32 by-the-glass via an Enoteca, plus an enticing array of exotically named cocktails. Sip fine French fizz at the Champagne bar while snacking on soft shell crab buns and other fancy bites.

GOLDEN LEAF, CONRAD HONG KONG ♟♟

Pacific Place, 88 Queensway, Hong Kong
852-2521-3838
ConradDining.com
Cuisine: Cantonese
Wine list by Mr Lee Watson
Wine on list: 530 (12 by the glass)
Wine prices: $$$
By the glass: HKD 65 - HKD 198

While the list is enthusiastically international in scope, most wine lovers will find it hard to take their eyes off the French and the Italians. The Rhone Valley wines and the verticals of reds from Piedmont and Tuscany are highly appealing. Half bottles are worth a serious consideration.

GOSTO, GALAXY MACAU ♟

Estrada da Baia de Nossa Senhora da Esperanca, s/n, COTAI, Taipa, Macau
853 28880888
www.galaxyentertainment.com
Cuisine: Contemporary Portuguese Macanese
Wine list by Mr Eugene Tan
Wine on list: 762 (10 by the glass)
Wine prices: $$$
By the glass: MOP 35 - MOP 98

Gosto pays homage to Portugal supported by a plethora of marquee wines under its various 'Collections' from Drouhin to Margaux, Tenuta Dell'Ornellaia to Felton Road. Possibly the real action follows these introductory lists. A tricky list to navigate, take your time. And leave room for the Ports!

GRILL 79 ♟♟♟

No.1 Jianguomenwai Avenue, Beijing , Beijing 100004
8610 6505 2299
http://www.shangri-la.com/beijing/chinaworldsummitwing/dining/restaurants/grill-79/
Cuisine: Contemporary Western
Wine list by Mr Max Hohenwarter
Wine on list: 620 (23 by the glass)
Wine prices: $

Immediately appealing for it's balance of new and old world producers; a good showing of Australia, New Zealand and South American wines from notable wineries. Classics of Europe aren't ignored either, but more affordable options are on show. Good list of Chinese spirits to finish, too.

GRILL & WINE , KEMPINSKI HOTEL TAIYUAN ♟

115-1 Changfeng Street, Taiyuan, Shanxi 30006
0351-8660000
www.kempinski.taiyuan
Cuisine: Grill
Wine list by Mr Zi Wei Zhao
Wine on list: 131 (17 by the glass)
Wine prices: $$$
By the glass: RMB 50 - RMB 198

Exemplary list curated with a clear vision to represent a global wine program, emerging wine regions and styles, and champion prestige wines and producers. From grower/producer Champagne to fine Burgundy and back to cult wine producers of Loire, Australia or Rhone, a very special and long list .

GUI HUA LOU, PUDONG SHANGRI-LA EAST SHANGHAI ♟♟

33 Fucheng Lu, Pudong, Shanghai 200120
86 21 6882 8888
www.shangri-la.com
Cuisine: Shanghainese, Huaiyangnese and Sichuanese
Wine list by Mr Neil Zhu
Wine on list: 100 (6 by the glass)
Wine prices: $$$

★ **Winner Best Food & Wine Matching List**

High-rollers are catered for with a spread of Romanee-Contis and classified Bordeauxs. For the rest of us, there's a moderate number of carefully selected wines with international repute. Plenty of food friendly options to match the refined Huaiyangnese, Shanghainese and Sichuanese menu.

GUINCHO A GALERA ♟♟♟

3/F, Lisboa Tower, Hotel Lisboa, 2-4 Avenida de Lisboa, Macau
(853) 8803 7676
www.hotelisboa.com
Cuisine: Portuguese
Wine list by Mr Paul Lo
Wine on list: 12780 (11 by the glass)
Wine prices: $$$
By the glass: MOP 80 - MOP 250

Of course you should head straight to the Portuguese wines on this mega wine list to get the true synergy of food and wine happening but what temptations are strewn in your path! This extraordinary 12,780 wines listing will amaze and delight. Truly world class. Just leave room for dessert (wine).

HENKES ♟

1E, 1601 Nanjing Xi Lu, Shanghai 200040
0086 21 32530889
www.henkes.com.cn
Cuisine: Mediterranean
Wine list by Mr Max Haahr
Wine on list: 83 (9 by the glass)
Wine prices: $$
By the glass: RMB 50 - RMB 145

 Winner Best Medium Wine List

A succinct, well-balanced list, that's complementary to the Mediterranean menu, which offers diners a snapshot of the world of wine. Respected producers sit alongside lesser-known affordable drops. There's a careful selection of whites and a more extensive range of reds – many with age.

IL MILIONE ♟♟

G16-21, G/F, Hutchison House, 10 Harcourt Road, Central, Hong Kong
+852 2481 1120
www.il-milione.com
Cuisine: Umbria (Italy)
Wine list by Mr Mesar Alberto
Wine on list: 380 (15 by the glass)
Wine prices: $$
By the glass: HKD 100 - HKD 280

Opened last year, Il Milione bursts with Italian gusto. With an emphasis on the food of Umbria we suggest you consider an Umbrian wine partner, the sagrantino reds look particularly smart. Italian wines are done proud, no better than the Tuscany and Veneto listings. The dessert wines are to die for.

IL PONTE, HILTON GUANGZHOU TIANHE ♟

No.215 Lin He Xi Road, Tianhe District, Guangdong 510500
86 20 6683 3636
http://www3.hilton.com/en/hotels/china/hilton-guangzhou-tianhe-CANGTHI/index.html
Cuisine: Italian
Wine list by Mr Arron Gwinnett
Wine on list: 100 (3 by the glass)
Wine prices: $$
By the glass: RMB 38 - RMB 70

A list that doesn't try too hard to impress with big names, but is crafted with attention to most of the world's great wine regions. That being said, a superb listing of Champagne and 'reserve' First Growth and notable Bordeaux is also on offer. Descriptions of each wine in the list is a delight.

JAAN RESTAURANT, RAFFLES BEIJING HOTEL ♟

33 East Chang An Avenue, Beijing 100004
8610-65263388-4186
www.raffles.com
Cuisine: French
Wine list by Mr Shuang Chen
Wine on list: 200 (12 by the glass)
Wine prices: $$

There's lots to like about a wine list that shows convenient, everyday kind of drinking list then steps it up to a 'Master List' filled with vinous gems, like a selection of fine Australian old-vine wines and plenty from smart Bordeaux producers, finishing with the rare Vin De Constance. Sharp list.

JADE DRAGON, CITY OF DREAMS ♟♟

Level 2 The Shops at the Boulevard at City of Dreams, Macau
(853) 8868 2822
www.jadedragon@cod-macau.com
Cuisine: Cantonese
Wine list by Mr Mathieu Gaignon
Wine on list: 750 (7 by the glass)
Wine prices: $$$
By the glass: MOP 70 - MOP 218

A sister list to The Tasting Room sharing the same wines but this time the food theme is Cantonese. An Aladdin's Cave for lovers of French reds and should the fancy take you, there's always the vertical of Mouton-Rothschild (1945-2009) to take home! Prices, as you might expect, are on the high side.

JIN XUAN CHINESE RESTAURANT, THE RITZ CARLTON SHANGHAI PUDONG 🍷🍷

Shanghai IFC, 8 Century Avenue, Lujiazui, Pudong, Shanghai 200120
20201768
http://www.ritzcarlton.com/en/Properties/ShanghaiPudong/Dining/jin_xuan/Default.htm
Cuisine: Cantonese
Wine list by Mr Henry Ng
Wine on list: 425 (16 by the glass)
Wine prices: $$$
By the glass: RMB 95 - RMB 360

It could be the back-vintage runs of First Growth Bordeaux, or simple additions like Mosel's amazing JJ Prum and cult producer Meyer-Fonne from Alsace, but this list is so dazzling with stars it's hard to decide where to drink. A prestige list of some of the world's great wines here.

JADE ON 36 RESTAURANT, PUDONG SHANGRI-LA EAST SHANGHAI 🍷🍷🍷

33 Fu Cheng Lu, Pudong, Shanghai 200120
(86 21) 6882 8888 ext 280
www.shangri-la.com
Cuisine: French
Wine list by Mr Henry Zhou
Wine on list: 450 (17 by the glass)
Wine prices: $$$

The triumvirate of lavish décor, a spectacular Cantonese menu and a truly global wine list makes for a top notch dining experience. The wine list spans the globe, with a surprisingly extensive Italian collection and a healthy spread of Bordeaux's. The new world is well represented.

JING'AN RESTAURANT, THE PuLI HOTEL AND SPA 🍷🍷🍷

1 ChangDe Road, JingAn District, Shanghai 200040
+86 21 2216 6988
www.jinganrestaurant.com
Cuisine: Continental
Wine list by Miss Wong Fion
Wine on list: 327 (28 by the glass)
Wine prices: $$$
By the glass: RMB 85 - RMB 230

The eccentric note to this list matches the unconventional flavour combinations found in the menu. Sure, you'll find swish Champagnes, blue-blood Bordeaux and a swathe of global names. But also 24 wines-by-glass and some quirky producers. The odd wine need retiring but otherwise its great.

JINYUE FRENCH RESTAURANT, JINJIANG HOTEL 🍷🍷

No. 80 Renmin Avenue, Chengdu, Sichuan 610000
86 028 85506199
http://www.jjhotel.com/EN/Default.aspx
Cuisine: french food
Wine list by Mr Ailing Wang
Wine on list: 90 (9 by the glass)
Wine prices: $$
By the glass: RMB 88 - RMB 288

 Winner Best Wine List – Western China

Particularly appealing for its depth of French wine, but enhanced by the feature producers like Trimbach, Chapoutier and Drouhin getting some extra attention and offering their upper tiers of wines. Of course the Bordeaux listings are impressive, but Rhone, Burgundy and Loire hold their own too.

KAKADU 🍷

Shop 1104A, 8 Jianguo Zhong Rd. (near Chongqing Rd.), Shanghai 200025
+86 (21) 54680118
www.facebook.com/kakadushanghaichina.com
Cuisine: Australian
Wine list by Mr James Sing
Wine on list: 2012 (11 by the glass)
Wine prices: $$
By the glass: RMB 45 - RMB 70

Plenty of options at this Aussie restaurant and bar though you'll need to sift through the sand to find the jewels. Nice to see classic Clare Valley rieslings and Hunter semillons, along with the diverse regional spread of chardonnays, juicy reds and quality pinots, including some kiwi classics.

KARTEL 🍷

5/F,NO.1 Xiangyang Bei Road, Near Julu Road, Jingan District, Shanghai 200040
54042899
http://weibo.com/u/2627395474?topnav=1&wvr=5&topsug=1
Cuisine: French
Wine list by Mr Louis Lu
Wine on list: 200 (100 by the glass)
Wine prices: $

There a strong French focus at this classy bar, including affordable wines from the appellations of the Languedoc-Rousillon and Loire Valley, plus a few 'classic' reds and fine champagnes. As for the 'world wines', there's a succinct selection of quaffable drops.

KAZUO OKADA ♟ ♟ ♟

5/F, Harbourfront Landmark,11 Wan Hoi Street,Hung Hom, Kowloon, Hong Kong
852-37462722
http://www.kodining.com/
Cuisine: Japanese
Wine list by Mr Akihiko Nosaka
Wine on list: 1903 (22 by the glass)
Wine prices: $$$
By the glass: HKD 55 - HKD 480

Arrive at Kazuo Okada early to give yourself time to feast your eyes over this extraordinary international wine list. The drool factor is high. The exhaustive selection of French and Italian wines, particularly Champagne, leads onto to an equally thorough approach to the rest of the world.

L'ALTRO ♟ ♟

10/F, The L.Place, No. 139 Queen's Road Central, Central, Hong Kong
852 2555 9100
www.laltro.hk
Cuisine: Italian
Wine list by Mr Derek Li
Wine on list: 550 (21 by the glass)
Wine prices: $$$
By the glass: HKD 118 - HKD 248

A solid list concentrating on Italian wines to match L'Altro's rich Italian cuisine but also offering so much more. There's room to splurge: '97 Barolos, '82 First Growths are mouth-watering propositions or there's always a serious selection of glass and half bottles to fall back on.

L'ATELIER DE JOEL ROBUCHON ♟ ♟ ♟

Shop 401, 4/F, The Landmark, Central, Hong Kong
(852) 2166 9000
www.robuchon.hk
Cuisine: French
Wine list by Mr Paul Lo
Wine on list: 3262 (17 by the glass)
Wine prices: $$$
By the glass: HKD 210 - HKD 560
> **Winner Wine List of the Year – Hong Kong – Macau - Taiwan**
> **Winner Best Independent Restaurant List**
> **Winner Best Wine List – Hong Kong**

A glittering subset of the great cellar found at the Grand Lisboa Hotel. Multiple vintages of the world's best wines with critics' scores listed as a guide. There's a heady list of French classic plus numerous new world and Italian reds. A sensational wine by-the-glass selection – 18 in total.

LE MOÛT RESTAURANT ♟ ♟

No.59, Cunzhong Street, Taichung , Taiwan
+886-4-23753002
www.lemout.com
Cuisine: French
Wine list by Mr Thomas Ho
Wine on list: 550 (20 by the glass)
Wine prices: $$$

Sommelier Thomas Ho has built a strong wine list of French wines with emphasis on some of the better value labels. The selection of Premier Crus, for instance, shows a particularly rich seam of gems at fair prices. And you'll definitely want to leave room for the 1957 Boal by the glass!

LI XUAN CHINESE RESTAURANT, THE RITZ-CARLTON, CHENGDU ♟

269 Shuncheng Avenue, Qingyang District, Chengdu, Sichuan 610017
(86 28) 8358 8888
http://www.ritzcarlton.com/en/Properties/Chengdu/Default.htm
Cuisine: Cantonese
Wine list by Mr Luke Liu
Wine on list: 279 (21 by the glass)
Wine prices: $
By the glass: RMB 80 - RMB 180

An impressive list of Bordeaux neatly organised for connoisseurs is the highlight of a list that works a global line-up, selected for best winegrowing regions and notable producers from each. Italian wines are also well-selected and worthy of attention. Lots to drink here.

LIGHT & SALT ♟

Add: 6F No.133 Yuanmingyuan Lu (YWCA), near East Beijing Lu, Shanghai 200002
+86 (021) 6361 1086
www.light-n-salt.com
Cuisine: "Lao Ke Lai" Fusion
Wine list by Mr Brandon Ho
Wine on list: 95 (16 by the glass)
Wine prices: $$
By the glass: RMB 65 - RMB 150

Step back in time to 1930s Shanghai and drink fine wine in Miss Dings Dining room followed by an extensive range of digestives in the Library Distillery. The wine list has a contemporary edge, with varietal groupings, realistic prices and quality producers – the red section is particularly strong.

Link Lounge, Sofitel Shanghai Sheshan Oriental 🍷

3388 Sichen Road, Sijing Town, Songjiang District, Shanghai 201601
+86 21 3761 1909
http://www.sofitel.com/gb/hotel-6329-sofitel-shanghai-sheshan-oriental/index.shtml
Cuisine: International
Wine list by Miss Melanie Canou
Wine on list: 106 (28 by the glass)
Wine prices: $$$
By the glass: RMB 58 - RMB 258

An extensive list for a lobby bar. Over 30 wines by the glass, including 4 Champagnes, and a couple of basic wine flights – overall a good global spread. Study the list closely to discover some respected producers such as Jaboulet , Craggy Range and Alain Chabanon. Icons listed up front.

Lobster Bar and Grill, Shangri-la hotel, Ningbo 🍷

88Yuyuan Road, Jiangdong District, Ningbo, Zhejiang 315040
(86 574) 87998888
www.shangri-la.com
Cuisine: European
Wine list by Mr Tank Tan
Wine on list: 145 (25 by the glass)
Wine prices: $$
By the glass: RMB 45 - RMB 235

Listings of super producer Domaine de la Romanée-Conti are very impressive, but so is the overall depth of the list that sources wines from all over great wine producing regions. French wines are most important here, but luxury wines from Australia, USA, Italy and Spain also feature. Good drinking.

Luccio's 🍷

242, DanShui Lu, Shanghai 200020
862153520587
www.luccios.com.cn
Cuisine: Italian
Wine list by Mr Paul Hopkins
Wine on list: 50 (20 by the glass)
Wine prices: $$
By the glass: RMB 37 - RMB 108

★ **Winner Best Small Wine List**

Plenty to like at this neighbourhood eatery where wine can be enjoyed without breaking the bank. There's a personal selection of French and Italian wines, imported by the restaurant. Though the list is small, over half are available by the glass and there are helpful tasting notes for each wine.

M on the Bund 🍷🍷🍷

7/F, No.5 The Bund (corner of Guangdong Lu), Shanghai 200002
021-63509988
http://www.m-restaurantgroup.com/mbund/home.html
Cuisine: Modern European
Wine list by Mr Zi Zheng Xu
Wine on list: 300 (32 by the glass)
Wine prices: $$$
By the glass: RMB 60 - RMB 140

★ **Finalist**

Sensible, different and free of pretense - it's divided into a short and long list – catering for the regular fine-diner and wine buff simultaneously. Top international producers are in abundance, with quality rising to the highest levels. Also refreshing to see a decent number of Chinese wines.

MAYA Mexican Restaurant & Bar 🍷

2nd Floor, Grand Plaza Building568 Julu LuJing An District, Shanghai 200040
62896889
www.cosmogroup.cn
Cuisine: Mexican
Wine list by Mr Rob Jameson
Wine on list: 85 (11 by the glass)
Wine prices: $
By the glass: RMB 48 - RMB 68

A vibrant, friendly, approachable list with wines grouped by style. Prices are accessible and there's a good varietal spread by the glass. Most major countries and varieties are represented – including a solid selection of Spanish wines. Its like a mixed bag of lollies for grown ups.

Messina Il Ristorante 🍷🍷

5/F, Harbourfront Landmark,11 Wan Hoi Street,Hung Hom, Kowloon, Hong Kong
852-37462733
http://www.kodining.com
Cuisine: Sicilian Cuisine
Wine list by Mr Akihiko Nosaka
Wine on list: 1903 (22 by the glass)
Wine prices: $$$
By the glass: HKD 55 - HKD 480

A sister wine list to Yu Lei restaurant and Kazuo Okada Japanese restaurant sharing the same wines but here, they are asked to match Sicilian cooking. The Italian section offers plenty of choice, including Sicilian wines. For your aperitif you can't go further than the exceptional Champagne list.

MIO, FOUR SEASONS HOTEL BEIJING
♟ ♟ ♟

48 Liang Ma Qiao Road,Chaoyang District, Beijing 100125
+86 5695 8522
http://www.fourseasons.com/beijing/dining/restaurants/mio/
Cuisine: Italian
Wine list by Mr Wifried Sentex
Wine on list: 500 (16 by the glass)
Wine prices: $$$
By the glass: RMB 70 - RMB 178

A brilliant list that travels to the great wine regions of the world, but the highlight are the collections, unusually named Champagne Glamour, Nobles de France, Italian Big Boys, The New Generation and The Future - here the list shines with incredible wines of pedigree and interest. Dig in.

MORTON'S OF CHICAGO THE STEAKHOUSE BEIJING, BEIJING REGENT HOTEL ♟ ♟

2/F,Regent Hotel99 Jinbao Street, Dongcheng District, Beijing 100005
010-6523 7777
www.mortons.com
Cuisine: Steakhouse
Wine list by Mr Allen Wang
Wine on list: 247 (16 by the glass)
Wine prices: $$$
By the glass: RMB 135 - RMB 245

Welcome to Morton's Steak House the home of spa-tinis, vodka and gintinis and general "tini" madness. Oh, and some seriously good American wines to go with your steak and fries. Wine glass sizes are as big as Texas (six ounces) and red drinkers will be in seventh heaven. A strong, all-rounder list.

MORTONS OF CHICAGO THE STEAKHOUSE HONG KONG ♟ ♟

4/F Sheraton Hotel & Towers, 20 Nathan Road, Tsimshatsui, Hong Kong
852-2732 2343
www.mortons.com
Cuisine: American
Wine list by Miss Sylvia Lau
Wine on list: 278 (15 by the glass)
Wine prices: $$
By the glass: HKD 110 - HKD 380

An attractive list for Morton's steak-orientated menu with a red list that offers great depth for the carnivore attractions of the plate. By the glass is light-on, but a breadth of international wines goes a long way for interest, including a neat selection from Lebanon. Dig in.

MORTON'S OF CHICAGO THE STEAKHOUSE MACAU ♟

Shop 1016 The Grand Canal ShoppesThe Cotai Strip, Taipa, Macau
+853 8117 5000
www.mortons.com
Cuisine: American
Wine list by Mr Simon Graham
Wine on list: 145 (15 by the glass)
Wine prices: $$
By the glass: MOP 90 - MOP 195

The Morton's Chicago Steak House franchise concentrates on American wines, naturally, so dig in to those Carneros chardonnays, Willamette Valley pinot noirs and Napa cabernets but do leave room to explore the rest of this tight little listing. The European red wine contingent is especially strong.

MORTON'S OF CHICAGO THE STEAKHOUSE SHANGHAI ♟ ♟ ♟

Shop 15 &16, Level 4Shanghai IFC MallNo:8 Century Avenue, Pudong, Shanghai 200120
+86-21-60758888
www.mortons.com
Cuisine: American
Wine list by Mr Royce Ye
Wine on list: 300 (24 by the glass)
Wine prices: $$$
By the glass: RMB 118 - RMB 254

A sister restaurant to Morton's Steak House in Beijing with a similar wine list featuring American wines to suit the steak house setting but with nearly 50 extra wines. Here, there are more magnums and more Bordeaux reds to choose from which isn't a bad thing at all.

MORTON'S STEAK AND SEAFOOD GRILLE SHANGHAI ♟ ♟

Shops 15-16, 4/F Shanghai IFC Mall8 Century Avenue, Pudong, Shanghai 200031
8621-60677888
http://www.mortons.com/shanghaigrille/
Cuisine: Steak and Seafood
Wine list by Mr Diego Zhang
Wine on list: 180 (22 by the glass)
Wine prices: $$
By the glass: RMB 79 - RMB 284

A balanced list with plenty of top wines to complement sizzled steak and seafood. Reds are up first, with a solid selection of American beauties across all main varieties. Assertive reds from Italy, Australia and Argentina are a feature, less so those from France. Some lovely wines by-the-glass.

MR. WILLIS 🍷

Anfulu 195 3rd floor, Shanghai 200040
54040200
www.mrwillis.com.cn
Cuisine: Mediterranean
Wine list by Mr Max Haahr
Wine on list: 78 (8 by the glass)
Wine prices: $$
By the glass: RMB 55 - RMB 95

Soak up the convivial ambience of this modern eatery while sipping on one of the carefully selected wines. The restaurant has specially imported many of the labels so you will find some new and different wines to enjoy. Decent selections from Spain, Italy, France, Australia and New Zealand.

NAPA WINE BAR & KITCHEN 🍷🍷🍷

2F, 22 Zhongshan Dong Er Road, near Xin Yong'An Road, Shanghai 200002
8621 63180057
www.napawinebarandkitchen.com
Cuisine: Contemporary Continental
Wine list by Mr Edward Kok Seng Lee
Wine on list: 694 (42 by the glass)
Wine prices: $$$
By the glass: RMB 55 - RMB 1680

 Winner Wine List of the Year – Mainland China
Winner Best Wine List – Eastern China

Ever dreamed of ordering first growth Bordeaux by-the-glass? Napa Wine Bar and Kitchen has all five on offer, plus Opus One, Ch D'Yquem, fine Champagnes and a smart international selection. The main list is simply spectacular, with all bases covered, from the accessible to the iconic.

NENE 🍷

Shop 106, 47 Yonfu Lu, Shanghai 200031
021 6418 5055
www.nenechina.com
Cuisine: Italian
Wine list by Mr Santo Greco
Wine on list: 80 (8 by the glass)
Wine prices: $$
By the glass: RMB 88 - RMB 128

Take a virtual journey through the vineyards of Italy, just by reading the wine list. Plenty of affordable options to match the Italian fare, whether you're after something unusual, like aglianico, or something familiar, like chardonnay. Alcohol levels and regional details provided for each wine.

NO.9 GARDEN MEDITERRANEAN CUISINE
🍷

No.9 Jiansheliu Ma Lu, Yuexiu District, Guangzhou, Guangdong 510060
86-20-8376 6197
www.no9garden.com
Cuisine: Mediterranean Food
Wine list by Mr Ned Cheung
Wine on list: 196 (9 by the glass)
Wine prices: $
By the glass: RMB 55 - RMB 60

With Mediterranean cuisine the theme of the food menu, it's great seeing such emphasis on Italian and Spanish wines. Though a global list, excellent wines from Rioja, Tuscany and Piedmont anchor the list, and show added class. Neat Champagne selection too.

NORTH RESTAURANT, THE VENETIAN MACAO RESORT HOTEL 🍷

Estrada da Baia de. N.Senhora da Esperanca s/n, Taipa, Macau
853 8118 9980
www.venetianmacao.com
Cuisine: Northeast Chinese
Wine list by Mr Jimmy Valentine
Wine on list: 592 (8 by the glass)
Wine prices: $$$
By the glass: MOP 40 - MOP 210

The heat's on! The North is home to some fiery chilli-led North-East China cooking so take care in your wine selections. The 592-strong wine list offers an intriguing trip around the world, lingering on Italy, France and the US. There's plenty of splurge targets so enjoy.

OCEANS, BANYAN TREE SHANGHAI ON THE BUND 🍷

19 Gong Ping Road, HongKou District, Shanghai 200082
86 21 25091188
banyantree.com
Cuisine: French
Wine list by Mr Ron Cheng
Wine on list: 210 (14 by the glass)
Wine prices: $$$
By the glass: RMB 50 - RMB 150

Oceans is largely devoted to serving seafood and so, it is to the white wine listing where we find some of the more interesting wines. Seek out the delicate white aromatic wines from Alsace, Germany and the Loire. Champagne is well represented too, including Lallier and Armand de Brignac.

ON56 - CUCINA ITALIAN RESTAURANT, GRAND HYATT SHANGHAI ♼

Jin Mao Tower, 88 Century Avenue, Pudong, Shanghai 200121
50491234 - 8909
shanghai.grand.hyatt.com
Cuisine: Italian
Wine list by Mr Zhong Fang
Wine on list: 235 (18 by the glass)
Wine prices: $$$
By the glass: RMB 75 - RMB 140

Wine sleuths will find some gems hidden in this list so its worth digging around. As always, be mindful of vintage – and price. A fair international spread with a focus on France and Italy including some interesting (and prestigious) cellar selections. A small prune wouldn't go astray.

ONE EAST, HILTON BEIJING ♼

1 Dong Fang Road, North Dong Sanhuan Road , Chaoyang, Beijing 100027
+86 10 5865 5247
hilton.com.cn/beijing
Cuisine: Modern American
Wine list by Mr Cina Houschyar
Wine on list: 233 (10 by the glass)
Wine prices: $$
By the glass: RMB 50 - RMB 94

The exceptional, mature cellar listing and a suite of fine, premium Champagnes, shines in a list that ably covers all bases from fine wine regions with a selection of established wine producers to some boutique offerings from well-chosen vintages. A broad list that offers lots of pleasure.

OPERA BOMBANA ♼ ♼ ♼

No.9, Dongdaqiao Road, Chaoyang District, Beijing 100022
010-56907177
http://www.operabombana.com/
Cuisine: Italian
Wine list by Mr Danny Allegretti
Wine on list: 900 (21 by the glass)
Wine prices: $$
By the glass: RMB 68 - RMB 198

Winner Best New Wine List

A broad list of Italian wines that covers the whole country, with some exceptional back-vintage and feature producers included. Collections of Vietti, La Spinetta and Col d'Orcia, as examples, lend great depth and interest to this superb line-up. This is very impressive and original.

OYSTER & WINE BAR, SHERATON HONG KONG HOTEL & TOWERS ♼ ♼ ♼

18/F, Sheraton Hong Kong Hotel & Towers20 Nathan Road, Kowloon, Hong Kong
852 2369 1111
www.sheraton.com/hongkong
Cuisine: Seafood
Wine list by Mr Ace Lee
Wine on list: 1000 (54 by the glass)
Wine prices: $$$
By the glass: HKD 95 - HKD 480

Plenty of internationally recognised drops to suit the extensive oyster selection or the globally influenced menu. Champagne's a specialty and there's over 50 sparkling, table and dessert wines by-the-glass. Helpful descriptions on each wine takes the guesswork out of choosing an unfamiliar label.

PORTOFINO RESTAURANT, THE VENETIAN MACAO RESORT HOTEL ♼ ♼

Estrada da Baia de N. Senhora da Esperanca s/n, Taipa, Macau
853 8118 9950
www.venetianmacao.com
Cuisine: Italian
Wine list by Mr Jimmy Valentine
Wine on list: 592 (16 by the glass)
Wine prices: $$
By the glass: MOP 65 - MOP 400

Portofino cements its reputation as one of Macau's finest wine establishments with Italian inspired cooking matched by a stunning Italian wine list. Bravo! The Barolo selection is particularly exciting. Bordeaux and US wine lovers won't be disappointed. There's a good list of Chinese spirits too.

PRESS CLUB BAR, THE ST.REGIS BEIJING ♼

21 Jian Guo Men Wai Da Jie, Beijing 100020
+86 10 64606688-2360
http://www.starwoodhotels.com/stregis/property/overview/index.html?propertyID=110
Cuisine: Fusion Foods
Wine list by Mr Ting Shan Chen
Wine on list: 207 (16 by the glass)
Wine prices: $$
By the glass: RMB 85 - RMB 165

This is an impressive global list with a lot to like, from fine Bordeaux selections to grand wines of Italy with some excellent additions from Australia and USA. Wines aside, the spirits listings are deep and excellent, and don't miss the exceptional detail in the tea section! Diversity rules.

QBA , WESTIN XIAMEN ♟

No. 398 Xian Yuan Road, Si Ming District., Xiamen, Fujian
361012
0592-3378888
www.westin.com/xiamen
Cuisine: Spanish
Wine list by Mr Dominic Ding
Wine on list: 112 (16 by the glass)
Wine prices: $$
By the glass: RMB 65 - RMB 268

A small wine list it may be but there's some beaut finds within its pages including a creative wine flight, some up and coming Chinese wine producers and a tempting selection of Exceptional Wines from the New and Old Worlds. Check the cocktail list for a couple of Xiamen-inspired special offerings.

ROBUCHON AU DOME ♟ ♟ ♟

43/F, Grand Lisboa Hotel, Avenida de Lisboa, Macau
(853) 8803 7878
www.grandlisboahotel.com
Cuisine: French
Wine list by Mr Paul Lo
Wine on list: 12780 (20 by the glass)
Wine prices: $$$
By the glass: MOP 140 - MOP 400

 Hall of Fame

A stunning collection of the world's greatest - and rarest - sweet wines, white & red Burgundy (arranged by appellation) and Bordeaux. 80+ pages of half bottles, 40+ of magnums. Big reds from the new world, classy Champagne, ultra-fine wines by glass. Updated with new releases/auction purchases.

ROOM ONE, THE MIRA HONG KONG ♟

G/F, The Mira Hong Kong, 118 Nathan Road, Tsimshatsui,
Kowloon, Hong Kong
(852)2315 5888
www.themirahotel.com
Cuisine: Lounge Bar
Wine list by Mr Alan Sun
Wine on list: 32 (11 by the glass)
Wine prices: $$
By the glass: HKD 95 - HKD 175

The sister wine list to Room One with one major exception. This is a wine bar and there's plenty of pre-dinner action in the cocktail and aperitif list. The section on Whisky is outstanding. There's also the offer of a Scotch Flight and a Japanese whiskey flight, that is one well worth considering.

S.T.A.Y., SHANGRI-LA HOTEL BEIJING ♟

29 Zizhuyuan Road, Beijing 100089
010-68412211
www.shangri-la.com
Cuisine: French
Wine list by Mr Kun Zhou
Wine on list: 183 (20 by the glass)
Wine prices: $$$
By the glass: RMB 80 - RMB 190

The three 'Rs' here are Roulot, Ramonet and Romanee-Conti, and that's just the start of this epic list. A journey through pretty much every top-end, big name fine wine producer from France, Italy, Australia and further afield makes for a very exciting, very deep list. An exceptional selection.

SCANDANAVIAN AIRLINES - BUSINESS CLASS ♟

Objective Communications, Beijing 100022
861065682243
www.flysas.com
Cuisine: Airline
Wine list by Mr Oz Clark
Wine on list: 12

Renowned UK-based wine critic and television presenter Oz Clarke offers his selection on board the friendly skies of Scandinavian Airlines, a best-of of available wines from prominent international wine regions. Great depth in the tasting notes, as expected!

SCARPETTA TRATTORIA ♟

Mengzi lu 33, Shanghai 200023
862133768223
www.scarpetta.cn
Cuisine: Italian
Wine list by Mr Christoffer Backman
Wine on list: 72 (4 by the glass)
Wine prices: $$
By the glass: RMB 68 - RMB 98

Small, but notable - due to its impressive range of Italian varietals (and its delicious menu). Ordering by the bottle is best, as the by-the-glass list is tiny. Don't be surprised if this friendly trattoria beckons you on a regular basis – you can try a different grape variety each time.

SHANG GARDEN BAR, FUTIAN SHANGRI-LA

4088 Yi Tian Road, Futian District, Shenzhen, Guangdong 518048
86
www.shangri-la.com
Cuisine: Huaiyang Appetisers
Wine list by Mr Shin Michael
Wine on list: 18 (18 by the glass)
Wine prices: $
By the glass: RMB 70 - RMB 190

A very short list, but there's some diversity and interest nevertheless. Everything is available by the glass, which is also an attractive benefit of the listings. Muscat from China, viognier marsanne blend from South Australia and the uniqueness of some selections work in the list's favour.

SINGAPORE AIRLINES SUITE / FIRST CLASS

Unit 4303, 43rd FloorBeijing Yin Tai Center Tower CNo 2 Jian Guo Men Wai Ave, Beijing 100022
861065052233
www.singaporeair.com
Cuisine: Airline
Wine list by Miss Jeannie Cho Lee

Small is beautiful. Nine expertly chosen wines - Grand Marque Champagnes such as Krug and Dom Perignon, top Burgundy and Bordeaux, plus gems from Tuscany, Russian River Valley and the Mosel. The presentation of the list is elegant and refined and includes extensive descriptions for each wine.

SOCIAL RESTAURANT, ST. REGIS LHASA RESORT

22 Jiangsu Road, Lhasa, Tibet 850000
0891-6808888
www.stregis.com/lhasa
Cuisine: Western
Wine list by Mr Allen Wang
Wine on list: 80 (1 by the glass)
Wine prices: $$

Could this be the best wine list in Tibet? Certainly shows some depth with big name producers like Italy's Gaja and Chateau Haut Brion featured. Lots to choose from in terms of premium wines, but a neat selection of Chinese wines are found too.

SHANGHAI SLIM'S

House 26d Sinan Mansions, 523 Middle Fuxing Road, near Sinan Road, Shanghai 200025
64260162
shanghai-slims.com
Cuisine: American Steak House
Wine list by Mr David Begg
Wine on list: 100 (14 by the glass)
Wine prices: $$
By the glass: RMB 48 - RMB 88

Plenty of hearty reds to match your 'cut to order' dry-aged steak! Though if Boston lobster is more your style, there are some delicious whites too. A busy, vibrant, global list, arranged by variety, with a particular focus on American wines. 14 by the glass. Prices are very reasonable.

SIR ELLY'S, THE PENINSULA SHANGHAI

No. 32 The Bund, Zhong Shan Dong Yi Road, Huangpu District, Shanghai 200002
+86 21 2327 2888
www.peninsula.com
Cuisine: Modern European
Wine list by Mr Jean Claude Terdjemane
Wine on list: 389 (24 by the glass)
Wine prices: $$$
By the glass: RMB 110 - RMB 270

★ Finalist

Sip fine wine by-the-glass, admire the jaw-dropping view and peruse one of the most sophisticated lists in all of Shanghai. Meticulously organised by region, choose benchmark or emerging producers, from the world over. Burgundy, Bordeaux and Champagne all exceptional. Top dessert wine selection.

ST BETTY RESTAURANT

IFC Mall, 8 Finance Street2/F Shop 2075Central, Hong Kong
29792100
www.stbetty.com
Cuisine: Modern European
Wine list by Mr Antonio Roveda
Wine on list: 132 (19 by the glass)
Wine prices: $$
By the glass: HKD 45 - HKD 140

From first page of wine there's finery - a list of excellent Bordeaux producers that sets a standard for what follows. There's a mesh of New and Old World wines, from vibrant whites of New Zealand to classic reds of Spain with some choice selections of local Chinese wine. Wine Flights are great too.

SPICES WESTERN RESTAURANT, SOFITEL FOREBASE �wine

137 Ke Yuan 2 Road, Jui Long Po District, Chongqing 400039
86 23 6863 9999
www.sofitel-forebase-chongqing.com/6415
Cuisine: Western
Wine list by Mr Remco Christiaan Vaatstra
Wine on list: 165 (19 by the glass)
Wine prices: $$
By the glass: RMB 78 - RMB 210

Looking for good value for money wines? Look no further. St. Betty offers a small but enticing selection of wines at keen prices, notably non vintage Champagne and New World producers. Wines by the glass is an impressive cross-cut of styles and countries. Many wine lovers need go no further.

SUMMER PALACE, JING AN SHANGRI-LA HOTEL ♕♕♕

1218 Middle Yan'an Road, Jing An Kerry Centre, West Nanjing Road, Shanghai 200040
86 21 22038888
www.jinganshangdining.com
Cuisine: Cantonese
Wine list by Mr Jerry Liao
Wine on list: 328 (14 by the glass)
Wine prices: $$$
By the glass: RMB 90 - RMB 240

Another winning combination of wines from the cellars of the Jing An Shangri-La. France reigns supreme with an illustrious range of high-end Burgundy and Bordeaux. The rest of the world is represented by a strong cast of respected producers. Also enjoy Rhone and Burgundian treats by-the-glass.

TABLE NO.1 BY JASON ATHERTON, THE WATERHOUSE AT SOUTH BUND ♕♕

Maojiayan Road No 1-3,Zhongshan Road South,Huangpu District, , Shanghai 200010
8621 6080 2918
www.tableno-1.com
Cuisine: Modern European
Wine list by Mr Xavier Zeng
Wine on list: 100 (14 by the glass)
Wine prices: $$
By the glass: RMB 75 - RMB 105

For a small, understated wine list there is a lot to like. Wine lovers will be pleasantly surprised by the inherent quality of the wines. Try one of the hand-selected, accessibly priced red Bordeauxs. Or perhaps an Egon Muller riesling, Margaret River chardonnay or even a complex condrieu.

TAPAS BAR, KOWLOON SHANGRI-LA, HONG KONG ♕♕

64 Mody Road, Tsim Sha Tsui, Kowloon, Hong Kong
852-27338775
www.shangri-la.com
Cuisine: International
Wine list by Miss Yuen Yee Lam
Wine on list: 70 (70 by the glass)
Wine prices: $$
By the glass: HKD 78 - HKD 198

 Winner Best By the Glass Wine List

An eclectic wine list where the wines of England, Turkey, Greece and Bulgaria mingle with First Growths and icons. Good value can be found here, look to the Italians whites and Rhone Valley reds, but should you call for something special keep in mind the Domaine Leroy Corton '89 for HK$12,500.

TENMASA, ALTIRA MACAU ♕♕♕

Level 11, Altira HotelAvenida de Kwong Tung, Taipa, Macau
(853) 2886 8888
www.altiramacau.com
Cuisine: Japanese
Wine list by Mr Keith Lam
Wine on list: 650 (18 by the glass)
Wine prices: $$$
By the glass: MOP 80 - MOP 160

 Winner Best Wine List - Macau

Tenmassa shares the same exhaustive, quality wine list as Aurora restaurant with one major exception: six pages of superlative sakes to start. There is simply so much choice to be found here, that making a decision could prove time consuming! A good enough reason for a return visit.

TERRAZZA, GALAXY MACAU ♕♕

Estrada da Baia de Nossa Senhora da Esperanca, s/n, COTAI, Taipa, Macau
853 28880888
www.galaxyentertainment.com
Cuisine: Contemporary Italian
Wine list by Mr Eugene Tan
Wine on list: 762 (18 by the glass)
Wine prices: $$$
By the glass: MOP 68 - MOP 248

Just as you can order Dover sole, Norwegian mackerel, Colorado lamb and Chilean sea bass here, expect to see a similarly expansive wine list devoted to world wine (and that includes Thailand). Big names, sometimes with big price tags, sit side by side with some truly interesting selections.

THE 1515 WEST CHOPHOUSE AND BAR, JING AN SHANGRI-LA HOTEL, WEST SHANGHAI 🍷🍷🍷

1218 Middle Yan'an Road, Jing An Kerry Centre, West Nanjing Road, Shanghai 200040
86 21 22038888
www.jinganshangdining.com
Cuisine: Steakhouse
Wine list by Mr Jerry Liao
Wine on list: 320 (18 by the glass)
Wine prices: $$$
By the glass: RMB 70 - RMB 120

The wines are as slick as the décor at this upmarket American grill, where the signature Australian beef is the specialty. Quality producers are peppered throughout – highlights include swish Champagnes, top Californian and Australian reds and of course France – including a page of Romanee-Conti.

THE CUT, FAIRMONT HOTEL BEIJING 🍷🍷

8 Yong An Dong Li, Jian Guo Men Wai Avenue, Chaoyang District, Beijing 100022
8601085117777
www.fairmont.com/beijing
Cuisine: Contemporary Western
Wine list by Miss Lynne Chen
Wine on list: 160 (13 by the glass)
Wine prices: $$$
By the glass: RMB 58 - RMB 240

While there is a fine selection of Bordeaux and Champagne, the heart of the list is an innovative and diverse spectrum of quality wines from around the world. Plenty of full-bodied reds to accompany the modern western menu, which specialises in quality black angus beef and pure-bred waygu.

THE EIGHT 🍷🍷🍷

2/F, Grand Lisboa Hotel, Avenida de Lisboa, Macau
(853) 8803 7788
www.grandlisboahotel.com
Cuisine: Cantonese
Wine list by Mr Paul Lo
Wine on list: 12780 (13 by the glass)
Wine prices: $$$
By the glass: MOP 60 - MOP 150

Cantonese food this good deserves a wine list as lavish as the décor (complete with giant projected goldfish)! Thankfully the restaurant draws upon the vast cellar of the Grand Lisboa Hotel. Every wine wish comes true with mind-blowing selections from the world's greatest regions.

THE GRILL, HILTON SHENZHEN SHEKOU NANHAI 🍷🍷

No.1177 Wanghai Road, Nanshan District, Shenzhen, Guangdong 518067
+86 755 2162 8888
http://www.shenzhenshekou.hilton.com
Cuisine: Western
Wine list by Mr Joe Wen
Wine on list: 377 (22 by the glass)
Wine prices: $$$
By the glass: RMB 50 - RMB 148

A very impressive listing of wines from China is supported by wines from Australia, Spain and USA, though of course Bordeaux is exceptionally represented in this list too. But it's those other regions that complete the list and make it excel. Champagne is notably lengthy in listings too.

THE HOUSE OF ROOSEVELT 🍷🍷🍷

27 Zhong Shan Dong Yi Road (Bund 27), Shanghai 200002
8621 2322 0888
http://27bund.com
Cuisine: Continental
Wine list by Mr Yuan Cai Zhao
Wine on list: 1901 (36 by the glass)
Wine prices: $$$
By the glass: RMB 98 - RMB 380

There's no need to travel the world in search of fine wine – as the House of Roosevelt seems to have it all. You'll be swept away by the inventory of Burgundy, Bordeaux and Champagne – but also by the comprehensive list of new world wines. As always, keep one eye on price, the other on vintage.

THE ITALIAN LIMONI, THE RITZ CARLTON 🍷

3 Xing An RoadPearl River New City, Guangzhou, Guangdong 510623
(8620) 3813 6688-8619
http://www.ritzcarlton.com/en/Properties/Guangzhou/
Cuisine: Italian
Wine list by Mr Kenny Persson
Wine on list: 189 (16 by the glass)
Wine prices: $$
By the glass: RMB 98 - RMB 380

The list leans heavily in the direction of Italy, starting with a neat selection of Prosecco and working up to more premium fare from Tuscany, Piedmont and Sicily, alongside some neat international wines. The Cellar Red Selection adds additional interest in this focussed list.

THE KITCHEN ♟♟♟

3/F, Grand Lisboa Hotel, Avenida de Lisboa, Macau
(853) 8803 7777
http://www.grandlisboahotel.com
Cuisine: Modern Steakhouse
Wine list by Mr Paul Lo
Wine on list: 12780 (9 by the glass)
Wine prices: $$$
By the glass: MOP 150 - MOP 200

The mega wine list that The Kitchen draws upon as one of a number of restaurants within the Grand Lisboa complex has grown from last year to 12,700 wines. A most complete and time consuming read awaits you! Take your time, an Aladdin's Cave of magical offerings awaits. Icons and gems rub shoulders.

THE KITCHEN BY SALVATORE CUOMO ♟

2967 Lujiazui West Road, Pudong Xinqu, Shanghai 200120
86-21-50541265
www.ystable.com
Cuisine: Italian
Wine list by Mr Calvin Chen
Wine on list: 250 (10 by the glass)
Wine prices: $$
By the glass: RMB 78 - RMB 138

The strength of this list lies in the diversity of Italian wines, arranged by region, with a good spread from Tuscany and Piedmont. All other countries play a somewhat supporting role. There's a sound selection of affordable wines by-the-glass though the by-the-bottle offering is more interesting.

THE MEAT, KERRY HOTEL ♟♟♟

No.1388 Hua Mu Road, Pudong, Shanghai 201204
86 21 61698888*6322
www.thecookthemeatthebrew.com
Cuisine: Steak House
Wine list by Mr Tielin Hou
Wine on list: 190 (26 by the glass)
Wine prices: $$$
By the glass: RMB 88 - RMB 198

The quality by-the-glass selection sets the tone for what is a balanced and extensive wine list. Plenty of classic French and Italians, to complement the carnivorous menu, plus a respectable new world offering. Iconic Burgundies and Bordeauxs are there to tempt or tease.

THE PLUMP OYSTER ♟

Jian Guo RoadNo 171/169-301 Taikang Terrace, Shanghai 200020
0086-021-54183175
www.theplumpoyster.com
Cuisine: Seafood Italian
Wine list by Mr Chao Wan
Wine on list: 86 (7 by the glass)
Wine prices: $$
By the glass: RMB 69 - RMB 179

Enjoy freshly-shucked oysters, fine wine and spirits at this atmospheric oyster lounge. The wine list has been appropriately tailored to the menu, including a dedicated page on oyster-friendly wines, plus a spread of bubblies and light reds. A good selection of pure, bright, expressive whites.

THE PRESS ROOM ♟♟

108 Hollywood Road, Sheung Wan, Hong Kong
+852 2525 3444
www.thepressroom.com.hk
Cuisine: French-European
Wine list by Mr Max Poon
Wine on list: 123 (17 by the glass)
Wine prices: $$
By the glass: HKD 58 - HKD 104

A smart, exciting small wine list totally in sync with the French bistro theme at The Press Room. Gives life to wines from the Loire, the South-West, Languedoc and the Jura as well as the more celebrated regions of France, and looks to some of the more exciting wine names of today. Prices are fair.

THE PRINCIPAL ♟♟♟

9 Star Street, Wan Chai, Hong Kong
+852 2563 3444
www.theprincipal.com.hk
Cuisine: Contemporary
Wine list by Mr Senki Ma
Wine on list: 800 (21 by the glass)
Wine prices: $$
By the glass: HKD 55 - HKD 180

 Finalist

What an exciting and contemporary wine listing! Full marks for seeking out some of the smaller, more interesting producers in France and beyond. Bold and imaginative, the choices for Wines By The Glass are spot on making it hard to move on. But do move on! The back section is full of nice surprises.

THE TASTING ROOM BY GALLIOT, CROWN TOWERS, CITY OF DREAMS ♟♟♟

Level 3Crown Towers at City of DreamsEstrado do Istmo, Cotai, Macau
(853) 8868 6681
www.cityofdreamsmacau.com
Cuisine: French Contemporary
Wine list by Mr Mathieu Gaignon
Wine on list: 750 (12 by the glass)
Wine prices: $$$
By the glass: MOP 70 - MOP 598

The Tasting Room lives up to its name with a stellar wine list that reads like a Who's Who of the French and Italian wine industries. We sense a leaning to syrah and cabernet sauvignon grapes with collections of De Beaucastel, Chapoutier and Guigal particularly mouthwatering.

TOSCA, THE RITZ-CARLTON, HONG KONG ♟♟

Level 102International Commerce Centre, 1 Austin Road West, Kowloon, Hong Kong
852-2263 2270
http://www.ritzcarlton.com/en/Properties/HongKong/Dining/tosca/Default.htm#
Cuisine: Italian
Wine list by Mr Ali Fong
Wine on list: 890 (24 by the glass)
Wine prices: $$$
By the glass: HKD 120 - HKD 580

Bella! Tosca will make an Italian wine lover's heart sing such is its depth and breadth. The country is covered with enthusiasm by sommelier Ali Fong, who plays indigenous varieties off new stars like chardonnay or cabernet sauvignon. Half bottles and large formats abound. Mark ups are generous.

TRATTORIA CAFFE VERDI ♟♟♟

6/A High StreetSai Ying Pun, Western Districts, Hong Kong
+852 2559 0115
www.monteverdi.com.hk
Cuisine: Italian
Wine list by Mr Armando Osmani
Wine on list: 110 (12 by the glass)
Wine prices: $$
By the glass: HKD 68 - HKD 78

A brilliant Italian-only wine listing in perfect harmony with Monteverdi's home style cooking. Small, family-run wineries are in the spotlight with indigenous grapes, sometimes close to extinction, featured prominently. A kind of Slow Food wine list if ever there was one. Great prices, lots of love.

TRB ♟♟♟

No.23 Shatan Beijie, Dongcheng District, Beijing 100009
+86 10 84002232
www.trb-cn.com
Cuisine: European Continental
Wine list by Mr Charles Sow
Wine on list: 950 (15 by the glass)
Wine prices: $$
By the glass: RMB 88 - RMB 210

Winner Best Champagne List – Mainland China
Winner Best Listing of Chinese Wines & Spirits
Winner Best Wine List – Northern China
Finalist

Wow. Here's a list that shows understanding of traditional, fine wine and some of the more exciting, emerging wine regions, with an eye on the organic and biodynamic for good measure. Impressive in length and scope, an exceptional global list that dares to show some difference. Kudos.

UNICO BY MAURO COLAGRECO ♟♟

2 Floor at Three on the Bund,No.3 East Zhong Shan Yi Lu, Huangpu District, Shanghai 200002
021-53085399
www.unico.cn.com
Cuisine: Latin
Wine list by Mr Junbin Qin
Wine on list: 260 (14 by the glass)
Wine prices: $$$
By the glass: RMB 88 - RMB 238

It's refreshing to see a list beating to the sound of its own drum. The focus on wines from Argentina is relevant and exciting – there are some regional suggestions upfront plus a good range of malbecs. The rest of the list is commendable, with producer and regional spotlights dotted throughout.

VIBES, THE MIRA HONG KONG ♟

5/F, The Mira Hong Kong, 118 Nathan Road, Tsimshatsui, Kowloon, Hong Kong
(852)2315 5999
www.themirahotel.com
Cuisine: Lounge
Wine list by Mr Alan Sun
Wine on list: 42 (10 by the glass)
Wine prices: $$
By the glass: HKD 95 - HKD 175

Vibes is a lounge within The Mira complex boasting a small but highly accessible wine list coupled to an aperitif section devoted to, amongst others, Signature Liquids and Celebrations Shots. V-licious Champagne cocktail sounds particularly party hearty.

VUE RESTAURANT, HYATT ON THE BUND 🍷🍷

199 Huangpu Road, Shanghai 200080
63931234 Ext. 6328
shanghai.bund.hyatt.com
Cuisine: European
Wine list by Mr Edouard Demptos
Wine on list: 190 (19 by the glass)
Wine prices: $$$
By the glass: RMB 95 - RMB 250

Take comfort in the presence of the recognisable labels, with the list being stronger in reds than whites. Some dependable Australian, Italian and Spanish reds – or try a Gimblett Gravels Syrah from NZ. Prestigious Bordeaux for those who choose – though consider vintage carefully across the board.

WHISK, THE MIRA HONG KONG 🍷🍷

5/F, The Mira Hong Kong, 118 Nathan Road, Tsimshatsui, Kowloon, Hong Kong
(852)2315 5999
www.themirahotel.com
Cuisine: European
Wine list by Mr Alan Sun
Wine on list: 208 (14 by the glass)
Wine prices: $$
By the glass: HKD 45 - HKD 130

This is a wine list built around price or, rather as the management promotes "extremely attractive prices." They are, indeed, very keen, which will allow many a diner to go upmarket, maybe to Vega Sicilia, Guigal or grand marque Champagne - all very affordable from this strong cast of Europeans.

WL BISTRO, FOUR SEASONS HOTEL HANGZHOU AT WEST LAKE 🍷🍷

5 Lingyin Road, Hangzhou, Zhejiang 310013
0571 8829 8888
www.fourseasons.com/hangzhou/
Cuisine: Western
Wine list by Mr Jason Yin
Wine on list: 180 (11 by the glass)
Wine prices: $$
By the glass: RMB 110 - RMB 210

For discerning wine enthusiasts, or those seeking a fantastic complement to the fine dining on offer, there's lots to enjoy in this list. Highlights include keenly-chosen Bordeaux and premium Tuscan wines, joined by an intriguing and neat selection of local wines from Shanxi and Ningxia provinces.

WOOBAR 🍷

10 Zhongxiao East Road, Sec. 5 Xinyi District, Taipei, Taiwan 110
+886 2 7703 8766
www.woobartaipei.com/en/
Cuisine: Western
Wine list by Miss Vivian Lin
Wine on list: 77 (10 by the glass)
Wine prices: $$

A short tour around the world of wine stopping by some of the more commercial wineries mixed with the high end. Table wines on this tight list tend to be dominated by the New World but Champagne has its own substantial and thorough section. Lab mixology drinks to start look like good fun.

YAMAZATO RESTAURANT, HOTEL OKURA MACAU 🍷

Hotel Okura Macau, Galaxy Resort, Cotai, Taipa, Shanghai
853 88835127
http://www.hotelokuramacau.com/
Cuisine: Japanese
Wine list by Mr Marco Tse
Wine on list: 56 (0 by the glass)
Wine prices: $$
By the glass: MOP 450 - MOP 15000

Not a wine in sight, it's just wall to wall sake on the Yamazato listing. The good news for sake novices are the tasting notes provided on each and every selection. Aficionados are especially well catered for. Do browse through the liqueurs covering everything from pear to plum to barley and wheat.

YAMM, THE MIRA HONG KONG 🍷

G/F, The Mira Hong Kong, 118 Nathan Road, Tsimshatsui, Kowloon, Hong Kong
(852)2368 1111
www.themirahotel.com
Cuisine: International
Wine list by Mr Alan Sun
Wine on list: 35 (11 by the glass)
Wine prices: $$
By the glass: HKD 95 - HKD 105

A simple but attractive wine list suited to the burger-pasta informality of The Mira. Prices are keen and the odd little find like Two Paddocks pinot noir will surely make a wine lover's day. Wine listed by style helps the wine search go smoothly.

YU LEI 🍷🍷

5/F, Harbourfront Landmark,11 Wan Hoi Street,Hung Hom,
Kowloon, Hong Kong
852-37462788
http://www.kodining.com
Cuisine: Shanghai Cuisine
Wine list by Mr Akihiko Nosaka
Wine on list: 1903 (22 by the glass)
Wine prices: $$$
By the glass: HKD 55 - HKD 480

 **Winner Best Champagne List – Hong Kong –
Macau - Taiwan**

*There are some mighty adventurous food tastes here: pig's
stomach, chicken kidney and pork intestine that may see diners
heading for the Chinese spirits or Japanese sake listings (which
are excellent). Otherwise, this exceptional list is up to the task
with an exhaustive array of top world wines.*

ZEST, THE RITZ-CARLTON, TIANJIN 🍷🍷

No. 167 Dagubei Road, Heping District, Tianjin 300040
(86 22) 58578888
www.ritzcarlton.cn
Cuisine: Chinese, Italian, Japanese
Wine list by Mr Mark Dong
Wine on list: 300 (15 by the glass)
Wine prices: $$
By the glass: RMB 120 - RMB 180

*Impressive for many reasons, even beyond the 'Grand Cru
Classe' section of the list that showcases some of the world
great wines. Depth of wines from Argentina, USA and Italy are
eye-catching, as are gems from cult producer Domaine Prieur
Roch. Balanced and exciting list.*

ZI YAT HEEN, FOUR SEASONS HOTEL MACAU 🍷🍷

Estrada da Baía de N. Senhora da Esperança, S/NTaipa, Macau
853 2881-8818
http://www.fourseasons.com
Cuisine: Cantonese
Wine list by Miss Hedi Lao
Wine on list: 1200 (12 by the glass)
Wine prices: $$$
By the glass: MOP 85 - MOP 240

*An established wine list that confidently presents a range of
fine French wines with strong support from Europe. Some of
the best value can be found among the Premier Crus. Good to
see Beaujolais and sparkling reds embraced, great company
for Cantonese cooking.*

For trade visitors only
仅对专业观众开放

ProWine CHINA

www.prowinechina.com

纷繁体验
专业品鉴

THE WORLD'S LEADING INTERNATIONAL TRADE FAIR
FOR WINES AND SPIRITS IN SHANGHAI CHINA
全球领先的葡萄酒和烈酒贸易展览会登陆中国上海

2014.11.12–14
SHANGHAI NEW INTERNATIONAL EXPO CENTRE
上海新国际博览中心

Messe Düsseldorf (Shanghai) Co., Ltd.
杜塞尔多夫（上海）有限公司

Units 307 - 308, Tower 1
German Centre for Industry and Trade Shanghai
88 Keyuan Road Zhangjiang Hi - Tech Park
Pudong, Shanghai 201203, P. R. China
中国上海市浦东新区张江高科技园区
科苑路88号上海德意志工商中心1号楼308室
Tel 电话: +86 21 6169 8300 ext.8311
Fax 传真: +86 21 6169 8301
Email 电邮: josh.gu@mds.cn
Contact 联系人: Josh Gu 顾建勋 先生

China International Exhibitions Ltd
华汉国际会议展览（上海）有限公司

Room 2402 Singular Mansion
No 318-322 Xian Xia Road
Shanghai 200336 China
中国上海市仙霞路318-322号
鑫达大厦2402室
Tel 电话: +86 21 6209 5209
Fax 传真: +86 21 6209 5210
Email 电邮: iris@chinaallworld.com
Contact 联系人: Iris Zhi 支祯珍 女士

Messe Düsseldorf GmbH

Messe Duesseldorf GmbH
P.O.B 10 10 06
D-40001 Duesseldorf
Germany
Tel 电话: +49(0) 211/4560-7788
Fax 传真: +49(0) 211/4560-877788
Email 电邮: BerlemannM@messe-duesseldorf.de
Contact 联系人: Marius Berlemann

Overseas Exhibition Services Ltd

12th floor Westminster Tower
3 Albert Embankment
London SE1 7SP UK
Tel 电话: +44(0)20 7840 2145
Fax 传真: +44(0)20 7840 2111
Email 电邮: fhawkes@oesallworld.com
Contact 联系人: Fraser Hawkes

Supported by 支持方：

Organized by 主办方：

INDEX 附录

图书在版编目（CIP）数据

中国葡萄酒餐厅指南. 2014 / 中国年度酒单大奖评
委会撰. — 北京 ：北京美术摄影出版社，2014. 9
  ISBN 978-7-80501-697-9

  Ⅰ. ①中… Ⅱ. ①中… Ⅲ. ①葡萄酒—酒吧—中国—
指南 Ⅳ. ①F719. 3

  中国版本图书馆CIP数据核字 (2014) 第209863号

策　　划：GOODLiFE MEDIA 范庭略
责任编辑：钱　颖
助理编辑：王新博
责任印制：彭军芳
美术设计：何　颖
翻　　译：孙　萌

中国葡萄酒餐厅指南 2014
ZHONGGUO PUTAOJIU CANTING ZHINAN 2014
中国年度酒单大奖评委会　撰

出　　版　北京出版集团公司
　　　　　北京美术摄影出版社
地　　址　北京北三环中路 6 号
邮　　编　100120
网　　址　www.bph.com.cn
总发行　　北京出版集团公司
发　　行　京版北美（北京）文化艺术传媒有限公司
经　　销　新华书店
印　　刷　中华商务联合印刷（广东）有限公司
版　　次　2014 年 9 月第 1 版第 1 次印刷
开　　本　150 毫米 ×212 毫米 1/32
印　　张　6. 7
字　　数　90 千字
书　　号　ISBN 978-7-80501-697-9
定　　价　49. 00 元
质量监督电话　010-58572393